Adriaan Bekman
The Mystery of Leadership

ADRIAAN BEKMAN

The Mystery of Leadership

alertverlag.

bücher auf der höhe der zeit

Translated from Dutch to English
by Els Klijnsma

Bibliografische Information der Deutschen Nationalbibliothek

Die Deutsche Nationalbibliothek verzeichnet diese Publikation in der Deutschen Nationalbibliografie; detaillierte bibliografische Daten sind im Internet über http://dnb.d-nb.de abrufbar

© Alert-Verlag, Berlin • Eine Marke der Frieling & Huffmann GmbH
www.alert-verlag.de • Rheinstraße 46 • D–12161 Berlin • Tel. +49(0)30 766 999 80

ISBN 978-3-941136-48-9 • 1. Auflage 2017 • Auch als E-Book erhältlich (ISBN 978-3-941136-47-2).
Gestaltung: Michael Reichmuth, Berlin
Sämtliche Rechte vorbehalten • Printed in Germany

My leadership motto

Doing the good in freedom
Out of love towards others
In respect for all that is.

Adriaan Bekman

For my IMO colleagues

Table of contents

Intro

Leadership is a fascinating theme full of secrets. There are numerous publications on this subject with so many interesting approaches but I maintain the opinion that leadership is still a secret, a mystery. In years of research into leadership, in which I worked with many leaders on the topic of their leadership, hardly ever a theory was mentioned but every leader had a completely personal point of view with regards to his or her leadership.

I also noticed that authors who have written about leadership, famous ones like Covey or Kotter but also more unknown authors, have based their leadership theory or model on a personally chosen starting point such as trust or communication between leadership giver and leadership taker, or ways to create added value and achieve results, or changes and initiatives to realize innovations, or the difference between being a manager and being a leader. Leadership, I concluded, is based on acquired personal capital. You can only lead yourself and others on the basis of what you have acquired yourself and you can only describe it by means of a starting point chosen by yourself, which ultimately leads to a specific leadership model.

This could mean that it is not worthwhile to write another book about leadership itself, which ends in a model or theory. However, I have noticed that there is a clear link between the proper functioning of an organization as a community and good leadership. Moreover, there is no recipe to be found which naturally leads to the good result. Entirely different ways of exerted leadership in different types of organizations can succeed or fail.

All this has meant that at first I saw leadership as a process in the organization to lead work and development processes, much more than a model or theory of leadership that focuses on the performance of the leader. Just as there are many taxi drivers that drive taxis in many places in the world and do this in different ways and there are many theories to be invented about the taxi ride, there are also different leadership processes in various organizations in the world and there are leaders who do this in their own ways.

It has also gradually become clear to me that leadership has everything to do with the moral questions that we must ask ourselves today. Leadership is a predisposing power at work; it is a force that works in the community. Leadership has to do with meaningful questions, the 'why question' has to be asked and these questions we can no longer hand over to the single leader who destines our fate. We are all part of leadership today.

This idea has made me perceive far more closely the dimensions of a leadership process and of the moral character of leadership that appear in organizations of a completely different nature, with different tasks and in many countries in the world, of different cultures and places in society. So I want to report in this book on the leadership issue in the following manner.

First, I noticed that leadership is traditionally shown in traditional communities such as families or nations or religions and that today it is shown in organized contexts in which we work and often also live.

In the natural community leadership is bound to the fixed laws of nature as natural succession of son to father or of daughter to mother. The leadership pursues there to continue the natural community with its traditions and customs. In contrast, the organized community leadership is rather connected with management and functional tasks and basically everybody can come into this leadership by taking part in the leadership process of the organization. Moreover, the organized community is in permanent change. We will focus on this distinction between the natural leadership process and the organized leadership process in *Chapter 1*.

The question is how we can investigate leadership as we recognize that it is still a mystery and we do not know exactly how it works. We have come on to two research paths that have to do with our ways of thinking. The first way is the way of the cause-effect logic and the purpose-means thinking, a thinking that looks at the patterns of things, finding an explanation of the meaning of being, as it also wants to be a basis for creating our own things. This road leads to theories and models. The other way we call thinking in balanced multi-dimensional realities. This is an inter-subjective way that is appropriate for the study of our own social creations, especially of anything that has to do with the organized life we lead today. This thinking is a creative thinking that makes sense of how things appear to us.

We examine leadership using the balanced multi-dimensional reality thinking. We will work this out in *Chapter 2*.

Then I noticed that leadership in organizations functions well as a process when three conditions are met.

The first condition is that the finally responsible person (s) has an inspired vision on the fortunes of the organization, a vision that is connected to the core task of this organization. This vision is connected to values which are largely shared in the community population and which correspond to what is pursued in its surroundings.

The second condition is that the managers of the organization are both able to fulfil their functional, professional responsibility and are willing and able to work together when it comes to changes and innovations.

The third condition is that the professionals of the organization are focused on their customers and serve them in their own way with specific products and services and that they do constantly improve their own work process and to that end are in a constant learning attitude.

If these three conditions come together, when this is the inspiring vision of the top related to the horizontal co-operative practices of the managers, and also connected to the professionals who make up the core of the client process, then these organizations thrive. If they do not, then the organization has serious problems to find the next steps in its existence. In *Chapter 3* we will examine this in more depth.

When we look at the history of leadership during the many centuries that mankind has lived in a community context and later in an organized context, we see three archetypes of leadership that dominate the community context and destine the fate of the community. These three archetypes appearing in the course of time we still see at work in the leadership process today.

The first archetype is that of the initiate leader who with clairvoyance can observe the fate of the community, see its future and determine the sense of community life.

A second archetype has originated from the functional hierarchical relationships in which we live in today's social life. This has evolved today into a management system that controls all the contexts in which we live and work.

A third archetype is a new type that is socially emerging in organizations. That is the personal leadership of everyone. Anyone can participate in the leadership, positioned between customer and supplier, owner and co-workers / employees. The world is becoming more complex so that everyone who participates in it has to show leadership on the spot, in the process, in the situation where he or she is acting.

These three archetypes of leadership are today at work in our organized life. They will be discussed in *Chapter 4*.

Leadership as a process emerges out of fundamental polarities that hold the organization as a living organism. The leadership handles these polarities and that needs different leadership qualities. We describe in *Chapter 5* four-leadership qualities connected to the horizontal leadership process.

Leadership is connected to community. When we focus on community and explore the communities of entirely different natures that we can see today, we can also come closer to the different dimensions of leadership as they can manifest themselves in the community. We will do this in *Chapter 6*.

Now we can address the perception of how the leadership practice today takes place. There is to my understanding a large gap between what we think about how leadership works that is shown in all those lovely management theories, and everyday practice in which leadership works or not and is displayed. A variety of practical situations can show this. We will have to come urgently to a more fundamental vision on leadership in the broad social organized context to recalibrate our views on leadership, take it beyond the often simple strongman images or complex constructs such as a matrix construct that leadership must work in. This is what we will explore in *Chapter 7*.

A foothold in the research of leadership is to focus on the question of what moral attitude radiates our leaders. In it we find something that all times and all cultures have in common. How to show those qualities in the organized community and how are they accessible to me as a leader. That's about leadership-soul schooling. We will explore this in *Chapter 8*.

This leads us finally to the question of the future of leadership. What can that future of leadership look like? In what direction will leadership develop? It contains dimensions such as the organized community, sense-making, creating process, basic leadership values. Finally, we summarize all this together in eight tips. We will do this in *Chapter 9*.

With this study we aim at contributing to a more fundamental approach to leadership that provides the reference for everyone who wants to participate in the leadership. This leads to focus on leadership as a community process and leadership as a moral task for everyone. This vision brings together the leadership forces working in the organized community as they can help us to search for and strive "towards doing the good." This vision also can provide some guidance to all those students who not only want to master a profession but also want to show moral leadership in that profession. That will give us, humanity, a future.

Chapter 1

The nature of leadership

Leadership and community are two sides of the same coin. Historically we see the formation of natural communities. Naturally family generations continue. There are families and communities with a common identity and culture and they make them visible to the outside world. A fascinating world of people alive and living in local communities has emerged in the course of the centuries. The special feature of the natural community is that it allows people's identity and culture to be transferred to future generations. We can assume that these creations of natural origin carry the meaning of their existence in itself as evidence. As an oak tree is an oak and will not be a beech, a member of a nation of people will not be a member of any other nation.

In order to operate these natural communities traditionally leadership roles must be taken up in these communities by community members and are also passed on by heredity. Thus, in the distant past we first of all see the priest / leader appear who connects the invisible world with the visible world of the community. The fate of the community is in the hands of the priest and he destines the fate of the community and of the individual. Anyone who cannot meet the identity and culture of the community runs the risk of being expelled.

These traditional natural communities were strongly associated with the cosmic cycles and with worlds of God's and they made sacrifices to propitiate these worlds. The priest / leader was on another level of being, on the level of the initiate, the clairvoyant. That meant a hierarchical level, standing above the community in solitude.

After the human society in the Greco-Roman epoch 'came more

to earth', and gradually a gap arose between the community and the invisible world, leadership in the community was laid in several hands. There were mundane roles such as the king, the healer / doctor, the master, the army commander, the mayor, the entrepreneur, the philosopher, the official. The leadership became, in addition to its hierarchical relationship with the community, a functional relationship. For the different community processes there were specific leaders with their own competencies. These roles were transferred to new generations along hereditary lines. There were leadership families who started to control part of the community. This eventually resulted in ecclesiastical and secular groups, which held power over specific dimensions of human life and the human community. The final result is a democratic society where political power is shared and where the entrepreneurial power is embedded in organized associations that produce and consume.

Since we are now, after several centuries of developing a global economy, all at the service of all, and this service takes place under almost all circumstances between people, people of different natural origins, in different social roles, are creating a different kind of leadership, which we call the personal leadership. Anyone can get access to leadership. It is not only determined by heredity (we still have a hereditary successor to the throne), it is not only determined by the leadership of political / economic systems (we still have party bosses and big entrepreneurs), but it is also determined by each person who participates as a customer in the world economy, as an owner, a consumer, a professional, a supplier, a citizen.

We live not only in natural connections like family, nation, religion, but today we live especially in organized associations in a global economy and this as a consumer / customer and as an employee. From dawn to dusk, from young to old, we are included in this global context and involved in it with our own roles and positions.

Where a dime was never a quarter in the natural context, this is possible in the organized context.

In this regard, in the organized community we still see the reflection of the old hierarchical / functional leadership represented in a sense by the top / initiate / CEO who determines the fate of the community. Leadership and community are also represented as a management system and the management system defines how we function. At the same time now everyone is part of a variety of communities and networks and performs in them showing self-leadership. This complex social and personal life asks from us a personal leadership. It is no longer sufficient to be guided by the higher leadership powers or management system, but it is necessary to take responsibility for the choices and decisions you make, the roles that you play, the moral quality of your performance in it, the workings of your deeds.

It can allow us to realize three old ideals of the community on a personal level and achieve them between us:

The ideal of freedom, which is "I myself give a destination to my own life,"

The ideal of equality, which is' we do it together, work together and get into dialogue within equal rights and duties "

The ideal of fraternity, which is' we serve others and are served by others."

We are ready for a thorough revision of our usual images of leadership.

We see not only the great leader that brings the community to its destination, we also see the management system in which we all operate and in which we must learn to manage our existence. We see now and in the future the personal leadership work worldwide where people work together and live in the two community types where hitherto they could not acquire a leadership role and significance. Society will thus, apart from the old vertical foundation of leadership and community, create a horizontal foundation of leadership and community to respond to the grandiose ability of people to act out personal leadership in their own lives and together with others.

Chapter 2

The leadership approach

Leadership is an issue that is beyond our logical way of reasoning. We will have to consider how we want to approach this mystery of leadership.

When I was a boy of 14 and in high school at the HBS (Hogere Burger School) attending classes, we had one hour of mathematics and the next hour we had an economy lesson. In math class we were faced with numbers and logical comparisons: $a^2 + b^2 = c^2$. I racked my head to follow the reasoning of the mathematics teacher. In the economics lesson I was taught by an active wealthy lawyer who had set himself a target of teaching young people economics for a few hours a week. It happened in front of our eyes and ears: he showed some laws like the law of diminishing returns. He described the field visually where a farmhand is spading out weeds between the growing crops. A second worker is called in and the work goes smoothly, a third, a fourth, till the number of agricultural workers has reached a size where the next farmhand who is added, leads to diminishing returns. I enjoyed his examples and stories and was immediately fascinated by the approach. Not only to see that 1 plus 1 is 2 all the time like in mathematics, but that in the social reality at a given time that what is ascending the created value may work later in the process creating decreasing values. He also described how we could trade on the stock exchange. He did it with us, bought a share; we followed how the share changed value during the year and why this was happening like it happened. The lesson we learned was: only speculate with money that you do not need yourself and when partly lost you can do without. Take your loss, no whining, and consider what your next step will be. Two years I attended his economy class and this led me to decide to study economics. However studying economics turned out primarily to be dealing with mathematics and statistics, and so I finally decided to study sociology with specialization in business administration. There I came upon a way of thinking that was much more multidimensional reality thinking. For example we explored the law of self-fulfilling prophecy. If we strive towards something special and continue to do this with attention then something happens that can respond to what we originally pursued. It may appear different from what we imagined at first but it is what reality offers us an answer, it is something in relation to the topic that concerns us and we are striving towards. This has become a guiding principle in my life. That is to say that things do not take place automatically, but something that we can follow with attention will ultimately manifest something that answers to what we were striving at.

Eventually I think I came to understand the relevance of a distinction between logical thinking and thinking in relationships.

Logical thinking is thinking in cause and effect, is thinking in purpose and means. This thinking provides the basis for our operational organized life, for our existence. We find causes in relation to effects that we observe, essentially patterns that occur on their own. We use this logical thinking in our actions as a means – purpose thinking. Essentially this is a reversal of the cause – effect thinking. We want to go somewhere and mobilize the resources to get there. It's nice that the train from Amsterdam to Utrecht is actually going there, preferably at the specified time within the given timeframe.

I will call this thinking vertical thinking. Things are essentially intended, it is an existential thinking, a thinking that is capable of connecting our sensory perception to the essence of things, to their regular appearance, to get on the track of discovering the laws behind the phenomena. It is a thinking that enables us to come to the constructs in which our society can function.

As Arthur Koestler described it in his life biography: we can predict exactly where the star Sirius will be in a million years. We can plan and construct conform the criteria we introduced. However, he also said that it is difficult to predict exactly where his cook will be in about 5 minutes and what he's doing. Things go different then we intended. That leads us to consider a different way of thinking, soul thinking and that is horizontal thinking. That is thinking in relations, multidimensional relational thinking.

Multidimensional relational thinking is appropriate for the inter-subjective world that we ourselves create with each other and amongst each other. This world shows itself in the organized structures in which we live and work. In it we ourselves create linkages, constructs and give them sense. This sense making is a process in which people with different opinions, perceptions, actions and initiatives connect to a meaningful pattern and a meaningful animated existence. This can go in all directions; it can lead to something beautiful but also to something terrible. In this relationship thinking we continue to think about how completely different phenomena relate to each other and how these relationships can change all the time.

The simplest example is that when someone is asked about his question, the issue will change during the dialogue and hence the person can find a way to a further step he/she did not see before.

We can approach leadership with our thinking in multidimensional relationships. In my research on leadership for instance, I became fond of the ratio of leadership – community – sense making. Leadership is associated with community and it has a powerful effect in terms of sense making. A triad like this is then a good basis in this book for our explorations. In it, we aim not at speaking the truth, but look for a meaningful approach that can also help us to get into the leadership ourselves, to get home. That is the beauty of this thinking, it makes you gradually part of what you investigate, it integrates itself into your life, it is something you can share with others and it works strongly between people.

Multidimensional relational thinking is thinking in paradoxes and polarities. Where nature and cosmos are embedded in this world and life, it is the soul that withdraws the natural; the human soul may be the only soul in this world that is not harmonically embedded. It is no longer part of unity, but it arises from duality, the separation of body and spirit, the divine intervention, the Big Bang, to become a three-ness, an in – between. You could say that everything in the world of the soul lives in contradictions and tensions and not in harmonious proportions. This applies to our inner world, as we think, feel, and act; it also applies to our social structures that remain only if we care and maintain them, as they are constantly changing, losing their way, and in need of a new sense.

Where essentially the body and spirit are evident, are connected to the world, and thus controlled, this is not true of the human soul.

The paradoxical nature of the soul tells us it is not right, it is not what you think it is, it changes. A beautiful way of putting it into words is: the soul appears and disappears.

That is the game set between the poles body and spirit, just as the soul of the earth appears between the poles.

This principle – it is not as we think it is – has inspired us as humanity to a wealth of questions, to be explored again and again. With religion, art and science we try to build a bridge, to discover a sense, possibly to create a sense ourselves. That has brought us to a higher soul consciousness manifested in the language we speak, the memories we have, the conscience that is speaking to us, the encounter with others, the appearance of the "I" in the soul.

All this forms the basis for the way I approach the issue of leadership. It is an issue where one can move oneself towards, that we as mankind can become part of, in which each individual can stand up and appear. That is the mystery leadership.

Chapter 3

The leadership hypothesis

Based on our view that leadership is not suitable for a model but to see it rather as a process in the organized context in which we live and that we can approach with the multidimensional relational thinking, we have come to a view, based on years of observation, on the well-being of organizations and the importance of leadership in this. We see three basic conditions of moral leadership that have a major impact on the well being of people and communities.

These three leadership conditions are:
1. The top of the organization has an inspiring vision that is based on the core of its organization, which is the creation of value for the customer and correspondingly the creation of value for employees, suppliers and owners. This has to do with the impulse of the organization, and this in relation to pulses of the people involved. "We let the organization do what it is intended in essence to do," which is a good leading principle of the top leadership.
2. The management has their operational functional tasks and works in hierarchical / functional relationships. With targets, results are achieved. In the end the management system is arranged. This system does not have the ability to change out of itself. There is a need for something else to happen. When managers are willing to work together to address questions of change with a horizontal co-operation, when they are willing to test their own ideas as well as their

management operation practice, they open the soul of their organization to the new issues, ideas and approaches coming in. This requires the manager's personal leadership.

3. The professionals work with customers in the daily practice. They complete the core process of the organization, the process with the clients. When all professionals working with clients, both directly and indirectly as client support workers, spend all attention to this client process and are not drawn into all kinds of internal hassle, the organization will then be fully connected to the social context in which it is willing and able to function.

So if these three are in communication with each other, the inspiring vision that provides direction, management working together in operational and change processes, the professionals who serve clients well, the organization will thrive and so will leadership.

This hypothesis we want to elaborate in this book and chapter in more depth.

The top leader

First, we can indicate the enormous responsibility and power of the ultimate responsible person(s) of an organization, the top leader. If a person has the final responsibility, he/she overviews the whole, takes the major strategic decisions and directs the organization to future beacons and objectives. The top leader also radiates moral authority. What does the organization do and what not? In this sense, the organization is a living organism that is supported by the top leader together with the community of people who have committed themselves personally to this organization. The organization represents a pulse that is certainly delivered by the original founders of the organization and that must be provided by the leadership.

In this light I have noticed, having worked for many years with principally responsible top leaders, that what lives inside the inner world of the ultimately responsible top leader largely creates the context that applies to other stakeholders. If all attention goes out to gaining profit and power, then the organization will be characterized by its pursuit of profit and power. The other members of the community will more or less have the same orientation, which is needed to safely establish their place and role in the hierarchy. Although on paper every possible good intention is formulated, a beautiful mission and vision are shown, in practice there can be very different actual forces that have effect on the top leader's leading of the organized community. Management and employees have a nose for smelling this, a delicate look to see what drives the top people and how they manifest themselves in the actual judgments and decisions of the top leadership.

Peter Drucker once called the ultimately responsible persons of organizations the creators of culture in our society. Organizations are the institutions that determine the morality of our society, was his statement. Bernard Lievegoed once stated that entrepreneurs and top managers are like reincarnated souls of the ancient priest s/ leaders in times of economic dominance, they influence the destiny of people to a great extent.

We can ask ourselves what is a good attitude for an ultimately responsible person of an organization in relation to what the organization can do in society.

We know "that it's lonely at the top" and so we can begin by arguing that ultimately responsible top leaders need to rely entirely on their moral intuitions. Because they are responsible for the whole, they have a good sense of how this whole can relate to the detail. If they come to judge and decide, they have to connect the whole to the detail. To achieve good judgement it is of particular importance that the ultimately responsible top leader is surrounded by reliable fellow travellers who are able to transfer observable realities into insights, share the facts and do not soft-sawder him/her.

The top leader is responsible for the creation of sense in the organization. It is his/her role and task in everything that happens to ask the question of meaning. That is the "why question". From research we found that consistently asking the 'why question' is essential for the leading of a smooth operation of complex processes as well as for the good conduct of people in the process and of a good outcome. Meaning is linked to values and values are the landmarks, the beacons for finding the right direction and this provides a good basis for reaching good decisions. In the organization many are concerned with the question of the 'what' and also the 'how' question. The 'why' question is rarely asked. Yet it is precisely this 'why question' that connects people and supports them in the realization of their own contribution. It helps to do the work as a whole and to not only maximize one's own interests. It is also important to be able to ask this question at the beginning, during and at the end of the process. All too soon we tend to mix in all kinds of interests, themes, options and goals in the process, which stakeholders confuse. The 'why' question always purifies the process and helps us to focus on the essentials.

Meaning has to do with vision. What is the dot on the horizon that we move ourselves towards, what is the leading image that directs our actions, what are the goals we set ourselves? All too soon they are concealed by and connected to the management system in which we operate. Strategic planning, budgeting, 'management by objectives', dominate the scene. Henry Mintzberg has shown us conclusively that an organization thereby quickly moves in the wrong direction, a direction people think can be controlled. We cannot capture the future, cannot predict the unforeseen, and cannot predetermine the proper action. We can ask the question of meaning and vision in dialogue with stakeholders and see the direction in which we can move.

Ultimately, the top leader is the dialogic pivot where the important things come together. This demands of the top leader not to be isolated in the control room and not to sit in the top of the tower but to ask the right questions in dialogue with all stakeholders who have as their interest that the organization is going well. This requires of the top leader not only to operate in functional networks with celebrities but also to meet the unknown and the surprising and develop an innovative look and image of what this unknown that presents itself could mean for the organization development process into a more distant future.

All this means that the top leader himself should be in constant development. Again and again he needs to tear down his boundaries, to step into the unknown. That demands courage and determination. It is constantly dodging the comfort zone, while just about everything for the final responsibility is regulated, and that is the challenge. Resisting the temptation of power that leads to obedient bystanders, again and again opening up the soul of the organization, will mean that the organization will integrate new impulses that through many new employees can find their entrance into the organization. This brings the organized community further on its way.

So far I have held a short discourse on the role and significance of the ultimately responsible person, the top leader, in the leadership process.

The management system

We continue with the second moral condition for a good leadership process in the operations that is the management system. In the hierarchically functioning organization the management rules and procedures establish the way we work. Even in organizations that deny emphatically that they have a management system, we can nevertheless see this system at work. It is more comprehensive and penetrating than we often think it is. It is rare for a professional employee to constantly decide what to do and when only from the perspective of his own wellbeing. He has his professional standards, his routines, his boss and colleagues, protocols and prescriptions. The management system largely controls his/her performance. When professionals and managers can put in the required discipline, this may well contribute to the smooth running of the operational processes. The management system forces us more or less to do this. Financial processes, facility processes, personnel processes, logistic processes, administrative processes, what processes are not controlled by the management system? We are so familiar with the management system that we are hardly aware of how our behaviour is controlled by this management system.

The complexity of an organization increases as a result of progressive differentiation of specialisations, which then lead to specific processes, functions, procedures. Also the rate of change increases. There will be continuous innovations at a high speed as a result of technological innovations, cultural interventions and social context-breaking initiatives. We wish then to control these with a more sophisticated management system. The amount of protocols increases, new system requirements are imposed on the management for operations to happen. On a macro scale there is an avalanche of laws, organizations on a meso scale are flooded with quality and control systems and in people's personal life there are also fast growing amounts of apps, emails, and messages to influence us in how we operate.

However, it now appears that this functional, hierarchically arranged management is unable to implement changes in an elegant way when these changes are handled with the same operational management system, procedures and methods, as the ones we use in the operations. Research indicates that such change processes rarely run well and the intended result is not reached. Usually they fail and end in oblivion. One of the main reasons is that the separate functional units do not have equal interests in the change. It also lacks an intelligent methodology to achieve the required changes in organized communities. All in all it can be said that the changes cannot be realized along vertical lines in the household with the operational management in charge but that they would rather be done in a horizontal way. There must be cooperation across borders by managers and professionals, who are also themselves part of the change. Change is primarily a reflective process that is input directed: new insights and experiences first have to enter in our inner life before they can be brought out again. So it is not only external changes but also mainly inner changes that we are dealing with. This is in contrast to the operating system, which is output-oriented.

Basically changes appear on three levels of existence of an organized community. First of all, this applies to vision. Are we willing to shift our vision, to possibly choose other targets, allow other guiding convictions than the ones we are accustomed to? We hang on to the familiar and do not give up quickly. Secondly, it involves a change in the constellation of people. New generations can come in and older generations say goodbye. In particular, this applies to the leadership constellations, as Arie de Geus describes in his book 'Living Organizations'. In change, people that do not work with each other in the functional organization household, have to co-operate with each other in the change process. Horizontal dialogues contribute to the change request and the search moves towards new realities. Thirdly it comes to changing work processes. In the course of time work processes are congested by all kinds of interventions of specialists. Are all the activities in the process necessary, do we take the right steps, do we cooperate and take responsible decisions so that the work process is in a flow and can continue?

With these three interventions, a new step for the organization is in sight.

When managers and professionals are prepared to cooperate rhythmically together under the leadership of process owners, there may arise a new infrastructure in which the change processes are rhythmically set up, continued and closed. After the first steps have been taken and minor changes have been carried out, the process owners encounter more severe 'bottlenecks' and 'Engpässe', blocking the necessary changes. Structures may be outdated, policy principles are no longer adequate, but still the management hangs on to them, management teams do not work together, there are conflicts between departments, there are disconnected processes. These structural impediments can be addressed in horizontally led change processes since the functionally operating vertical channels are not suitable for them. The change processes can deal with much unresolved grief from the past that is cleaned up and brought to a sensible next step. In that sense, change also cleanses the soul of the organization.

The professionals and their clients

A third condition is the way professionals interact with their clients and suppliers. The staff/professionals are busy with their work process. Moreover, the employees/professionals become increasingly individualized and that means that every professional develops his own knowledge and skills and collaborates with many other employees and professionals both within and outside the organization. The work can be so absorbing that the eye for the client, the other person that we actually serve, is lost. The nurse is busy with her care and administration and the patient waits until she has attention and time for him. The accountant is busy with his computer and his own statements that are set up out of his special knowledge and forgets to give the appropriate financial information to the right person. However, it is precisely the client who directs the meaning of the work we do. What does the client do with my work, how does my product, service or advice work in his process? We may ourselves as clients too often experience that the person who serves us is very busy with his own process and not with us as clients. But we also experience the wonderful examples of people who do this consciously and with attention to serve their clients. It makes a big difference in life quality in the perception of clients and employees. In the process with the client, all organizational processes come together. In the client process the production, financial, personnel and marketing policy appear concrete in its effect. In the process with the client we can observe very keenly and meet all functional influences working in a good way or in a way in which they work against each other. This happens all too often.

How do we ensure that all the different professionals can still find something in common in their work? There is only one answer and that is the client of the organization on the one hand and the impulse of the organization on the other hand that can bring us together. It is essential for every professional to have a connection to these two poles of the organization. We can compare them to the north and south poles of the earth. These two constant poles give balance to all the turbulent events that happen between the poles.

Cohesion

The leadership secret we find in what is happening between these three conditions. The worst case scenario is when the three are not completely connected to each other. In popular terms: What occupies the minds of the top has little to do with the process that the management is pursuing and this has in turn little to do with what the professionals are doing. That this might be the case may seem absurd, but in my perception it happens in organizations quite often. There is a gap anyway between the world in which the top leader and management live who work in different layers in different places with different themes, and the world of the professionals who each have their own work in concrete situations and must act and represent them all.

I picture this sometimes as follows:

The organization is a table with chairs around it.

The top people are standing on the table and see what is happening around them. They can move across this table, as they see what is happening around the table and can give directions to others.

The managers have their own chairs next to the table the top people stand on. They see what the top is engaged in, they see their colleagues on the different chairs and they are bound to their chairs. They call each other things, and try to translate what is happening above the table down to the people under the table.

On the floor next to the table are the team leaders, grouped around chairs. They can more or less see what other colleagues are doing who are standing around the nearest chair and they cast an occasional glance under the table where the professionals are busy at work. They must ensure that things function.

The professionals are busy at work under the table where the customers appear and disappear. They are busy with their work process and hear the occasional shout of their team leader. They sometimes look just outside the table to see their department head on his chair, busy with other seat occupants. The top is far from them being very busy and completely out of the picture for the professionals.

The question is how do these people in different positions at different levels communicate with each other so that what they are doing is somehow connected to what the others do. That is what we can call the leadership process in the community: the process in which people connect with each other. Leadership gives guidance to people in a community.

This image of table and chairs also makes clear that leadership directing vertically is a difficult thing. It does not really work. Leadership works when stakeholders come together in a horizontal relationship. They come out of their social function and position, leave their table and chairs, and share what they see as real issues, share how to address things in their community and share what may or may not work properly. This horizontal conversation requires a reflection space where people can meet each other as persons and can enter into a dialogue on key issues facing the organization.

In my own experience the design of such a reflection place where people can meet each other with certain regularity is an essential ingredient for the proper functioning of the leadership in the organization.

In my work as a facilitator for leadership processes in organizations I've been tasked with setting up and taking care of these reflection spaces. It strikes me again and again that when people of different levels discuss with each other essential themes that play a role in the organization and when they are willing to listen to each other, this has a revealing and inspiring effect on all participants. All see very quickly what is nonsense in what is done and where there are opportunities to get to further productive steps. It is actually incomprehensible that so little use is made of this horizontal space. In small companies this is almost a self-evident matter because one is close to each other and there are short and direct lines between people. When the organization grows slightly larger than this 'the table and chairs problem' arises immediately; people do not understand each other. In large organizations directors dialogue with directors, department heads with department heads, team leaders with team leaders and professionals with professionals. They seldom truly work and dialogue all together. When they meet, then this happens in the functional-hierarchical way and not really on a personal level. Each person remains in his own space. It is therefore an illusion to think that all kinds of systems, HRM systems in particular, can escape this functional differentiation. Even the performance appraisal meeting between manager and employee is usually restricted to a functional exchange. The personal issues are left outside the meeting.

In summary, one can say that the leadership process will only function well if those involved are boarding this as persons and in dialogue with others come to steps and take them out of personal responsibility, therein linking top leader responsibility, management system and professional customer service with each other. It leads to good judgment building and decision making especially in processes of change.

Chapter 4

The history of leadership

A first substantiation of the hypothesis expressed in chapter 3 is found in the study of the history of leadership. The development of leadership is linked to the development of human society.

For many centuries we have seen human communities develop along a triple line.

The first line is the emergence of a theocratic society or community. In ancient times, first in the east and later also in the western world, theocratic communities arose. In them, the priest/initiate takes the lead. This person is responsible for ensuring that the community finds its way. The priest/initiate is able to connect the visible with the invisible world. From the invisible divine worlds come impulses that give the community its existence and direction. Conversely questions of life and desires in the community are presented to the gods.

A world of temples and sacrifices arises. The people are fully embedded in the traditions and they perform the sacrifices and prayers to implore the great salvation.

Gradually growing communities develop over a long time period into more skilful societies where the people accomplish the daily work and living processes together. The leadership comes to earth. It is not only laid in the hands of priests/insiders but also in worldly hands. This brings about principalities and even empires. The most obvious step in this direction we see in the Greco-Roman societies. Here shared leadership originates. There is political leadership but for concrete processes there is also a new kind of leaders such as the captain of the ship, the judge, the doctor, the teacher, the philosopher. A decisive step for the leadership is the creation of a more democratic society in which people want to take important decisions in harmony with each other. Parliament arises and directions for communities are given for parliamentary discussions. We now see the battle for leadership emerge. Finally we see the first real organizations coming into being: armies and churches. Army leaders/rulers and popes/cardinals dominate the scene. The army chief/king dominates the outer society; the Pope governs the soul, the inner world of people. The army leaders/rulers develop into presidents and bureaucrats and other rulers who arrogate the power in society. The faith of people is put in the hands of leaders of religious organizations. Church and state are separate and manage both sides of the human community. Leaders of both institutions have to agree to see it through with each other. Sometimes the Pope is a worldly leader and sometimes the monarch is also Pope.

Gradually during the last thousand years we see the development of a third phase in the community and leadership. People start trading with each other in companies over the borders of their own community. Regional, national and international socio – economic relations arise between peoples and organizations. There is a growing world economy and entrepreneurs take the power. They create a new world of relations in which business interests are paramount. This leads to the situation in which even kings and priests depend on the world economic powers.

Now we find in our societies an amalgamation of these three forces of community and leadership:

The power of the priest/insider who knows the soul of man and of the community,

The strength of the social order, rule of law, which regulates relations in the community,

The power of the organized world economy in which everybody participates, assisting and serving others.

Finally we have constituted a society that has realized these three dimensions in themselves.

Society has a cultural life of philosophy, religion and art that appeals to the inner world of people,

Society has laws to live with which regulate social relations, which make sure there is justice, and which allow politics to be conducted.

Society has an economic life of producing and consuming people in which the value creation will appear as product, service and advice.

Leadership has become a reflection of this differentiated society. Politicians, businessmen, cultural leaders, they need to find their way to each other. Each rules in his own field but should tune with others as the issues of complexity and morality arise beyond its borders.

We want to designate this leadership as a historical source; we can identify the following three images:

In the theocratic society:

Upper World

The leader as initiate

Under World

In the democratic society:

Upper World

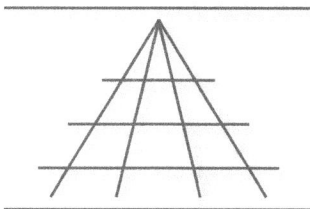

The management system

Under World

In the economic society:

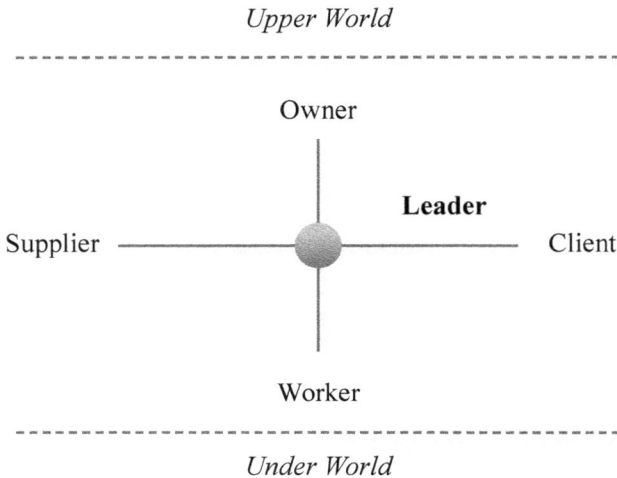

Upper World

Owner

Leader

Supplier ——————————————● —————————— Client

Worker

Under World

All three forms of leadership are active in our society. We find them in every organization.

It is still true that the leadership of the top leader means being the ultimately responsible person for well being of the community and that the fate of this community is largely determined by the moral choices and decisions of the top leader. The top leads the process of judgment building and decision-making and connects to all resources that can help to work this out. Where once the ultimately responsible top leader could draw from invisible sources, the leadership is now dependent on all sources that arise in the observable reality. The conversation and dialogue with the other persons involved gives the top leader guidance.

On the other hand we all become self-aware. Meeting with and talking to people as sources of vision and momentum and thus as our direction-givers for control and decision-making, all this is key to leadership. It creates the meaning of life for all and then all can act independently in the light of the whole.

It is the horizontal cooperation between responsible managers/ supervisors, working on the fundamental questions and issues, that makes the processes and communications flow as they break through the functional blinkers boundaries and remove hierarchical earplugs.

In the processes that the professionals act in, they can not just do the job and serve clients, but they can also participate in improving their own work processes. That gives the professional and the manager a deeper understanding from a learning experience. That gives fulfilment.

The professionals who focus on their client process experience the energizing effect that is produced by this client event. It is also the client, the other person we serve, who seeks the relationship with the supplier and this serves the personal connection, the mutual understanding, and the joint consideration of the different interests.

If these three:
- The inspiration of a moral vision at the top,
- The good cooperation in equality in the organizational set-up by middle management,
- The service to others with attention given by the professional,

come together, then the leadership is productive and gives the people who are involved in it a fulfilled existence.

Chapter 5

Leadership Qualities

We can characterize the organization as a living organism on the basis of three basic dimensions of life. These are the vertical, the horizontal and the diagonal dimension.

Plato already identified these dimensions in his description of the creation of the human soul.

First there was a whole, a round case, so to speak. That whole was split into two halves.

The two parts, a vertical and a horizontal one, were connected to each other in the form of a cross. Both vertical and horizontal part could make a circular motion in opposite directions. Between these two moving axes a third dimension was created, a living space, a soul.

We can also see these dimensions as polarities. They are polar tensions between which a middle arises. Ultimately the polarity ends in a triangle.

In this way I want to picture the main tensions that earmark an organization . This results in an image of essential leadership qualities.

The first tension looks like this.

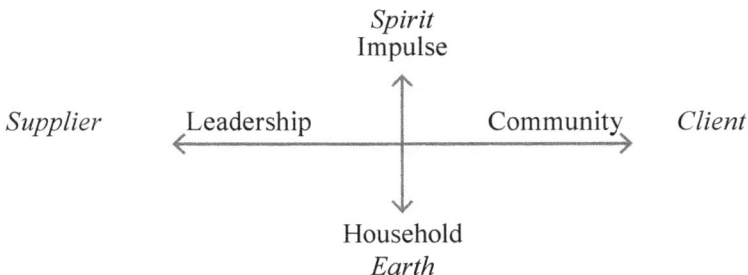

Supplier — Leadership — Community — *Client* (horizontal axis); *Spirit* / Impulse (top) — Household / *Earth* (bottom) vertical axis

On the vertical axis we see the polarity Impulse – Household.

The organization arises from an impulse that appears through a person or a group of persons. The impulse is an idea that is realized in an organ.

The organization takes shape and structure into its design. With the forces hierarchy and functionality or purpose this creates an institutional household that can realize this impulse.

On the horizontal axis we see the polarity Client – Supplier.

It is the need of a client, which can be answered with a response. The client designates the existence of an organization and in the process with the client all the processes involved in the organism come together.

The supplier is the person who has the expertise to create a product or service or advice that meet the needs of clients.

These two dimensions relate to each other through the leadership in the community. A community of people work on the processes in collaboration with each other. This creates synergy. The leadership steers these processes, it provides the dialogue and involves the actual people in the process of creating and working together.

The second tension is as follows:

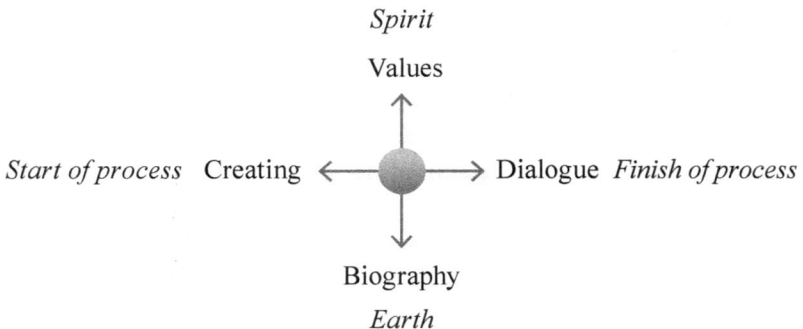

Spirit

Values

↑

Start of process Creating ←———●———→ Dialogue *Finish of process*

↓

Biography

Earth

Human beings and organizations write biographies, life stories. They are born, they go through stages of life going back and forth, and they die. Each biography is unique and also reflects phases and crises that we share as human beings. We come out of the cosmic spirit as man and arrive on earth. We penetrate the earth deeper to the point halfway when the biography slowly ascends to the spirit and blends with it.

As persons and as an organization we live a process, we live in processes. These processes take place cyclically repetitive, always in a different way. Processes of thinking and action unfold in time in operative and reflective areas. Processes of production, community and learning constantly take place in human affiliation.

These two dimensions are related as dialogue in a value creating way. It is a two-way traffic that happens economically as well as socially and culturally. We create economic, social and cultural values. They appear and disappear.

The leadership handles this tension. We call this horizontal leadership.

We can distinguish four key qualities of leadership that are important for handling this tension. They are the qualities that can help managers and professionals to act as leaders. They can be applied in essence by all those who work in organized associations.

These are the qualities:
- Giving direction to processes,
- Coaching of learning,
- Inspiring with a vision,
- Intervening by confronting.

Giving direction to processes

Leadership is a quality that should in the future be performed as a shared quality by managers and professionals. We described this as a leadership process in the organized community and as leadership as a moral category.

Leadership as a process is related to the steering of work processes and the sense making through reflective processes.

Steering work processes involves both the design of good work processes and giving direction to the activities, collaboration and decision-making processes. This work process focuses on the client and thereby provides a flow in the processes because it is rhythmically arranged, related to the core of the work process. Besides work processes there are reflective processes, which explore how things work and how this might be improved. Also these processes provide guidance to make the organization as a living organism exist in a vital way.

Coaching of learning

The ability of managers and professionals, their knowledge and skills as well as their attitude while practising their profession largely determine the quality of the performance of the organization. This requires continuous learning. Also learning together in the form of knowledge creation and transfer, the power of initiative taking by developing new ideas and shaping them. Managers and professionals not only have jobs to do, but they also have responsibility for their job development related to further development of the organization and society. The growing learning ability of people and organizations increase the quality of life and therefore better contribute to people and society.

Inspiring with a vision

Organizations work better when there is a clear vision underlying the direction it takes. That vision is in continuous development through a dialogue with all stakeholders. What moves our stakeholders and how can this be translated into an inspiring vision? This would include goals and strategy development. We will work with goals in mind and there is a continuous strategic dialogue with all stakeholders about the next steps to be taken. Now this is no longer an elitist process for individuals but a community process in which all participate. Here is the direct link with sense making and motivation present in thinking about the meaning of work, why the work is as it is, and encouraging the change for the better. This helps any person to think and act in the light of the whole.

Intervening by confronting.

Not infrequently boundaries get blurred and it is unclear whether or not what we do contributes anything yet. We get into habits and routines that threaten to claim our energy and attention, our time and space is occupied increasingly by things that may no longer be so important. How do we set new boundaries, how do we stop meaningless work, how can we create time and space for new steps, that is the question. This requires an explicit and constant attention to proper investment and proper cost cutting. These must go hand in hand. This requires a regular confrontation with the existing practice and the darling children of managers and professionals who actually have no future.

We all, who participate in organized life, can practice these four key qualities of leadership. This helps the organization and the person to be properly connected to its original sources and also to take a good step into the future, which in principle is unknown but must be faced.

Chapter 6

Leadership community

We can also explore the mystery of leadership by approaching it from the question how leadership is fundamentally connected with understanding community. Leadership and community are two sides of the same coin, is what I have argued. Community goes hand in hand with leadership and leadership is associated with community.

What do we mean by community?

Community not only expresses that there is a link between people, it also expresses a gathering of people. We are part of a community, but we have fellowship with one another, in the most spiritual and in the most practical sense.

The most intimate community is that of the *four-eyes community.* I go along with the other person; the other person is with me. In this four-eyes community as an intimate community, life dimensions are cared for. We love each other, read each other lessons, go on our joint way, we are engaged in a struggle. If you really want to create something in a relationship it is the four-eyes community that substantially works. At work it is essential for supervisor and employee to be able to dialogue in private. There it is you and me that it is all about and it should bring us together. Everything separates us as unit head and staff in the workplace but we know if it goes well when we bridge the gap between us in a good conversation.

The group is a different community. Here more people come together. Bernard Lievegoed distinguished the work group, the social group and the study/learning group.

People work together in groups and thus create added value. Here you can experience the synergy effect. Together we achieve more than each person for himself alone. People join a group and participate in the group process. The working group has an important place in organized life.

We are a social group when we meet and live together. Family, friends, the club, the team, people are together to experience something together and do this as an activity and for quality of life. The social group is strongly connected with the natural community life.

The study/learning group is a group in which people come together who want to take a common development step, learn from a common doctrine issue. This group has a strong karmic nature, it brings together people from different social groups and they learn together and develop themselves in consciousness.

A folk society was originally a community of people that share natural sources, from blood and soil, from a common lineage and they share life together. Coming out of heredity, religion, culture, the rituals and traditions play an important role in the community life.

An organization is an organized community. A common goal unites us. We strive to support other people, our clients, and we do this as an organized community in a hierarchical-functional relationship. In an organization people with completely different backgrounds, beliefs, trainings and what not, still work well for years and live together. Everything is directed outwards, the inner world of the organization needs to adapt constantly to that surrounding world.

An ideal community is a community of people living in different parts of the world; an ideal connects them together as an important part of their lives. They may not even know each other but they execute the same process and give it more or less the same meaning. The modern media support the emergence of these communities that we did not know before.

So we are as people stretched over many communities and this unfolds our lives.

I want to reflect more closely on three different types of communities and explore how leadership plays a role in them. These types of different communities can appear as four-eyes communities, groups, folk societies, organized associations and ideal communities.

These three communities are:

The natural community,
The organized community,
The individual community.

The natural community

People live in natural communities. These communities survive from heredity. You are born into, live in and die in this natural community. In moments of birth and death, of marriage, illness and healing, learning and initiation, in these moments the natural community is connected around the step that individuals take.

From the natural community no one can escape. Your parents are your parents, your family is your family, your faith and spirituality is your faith and spirituality. Any attempt to abandon them is smothered in the physical fact.

Natural communities are basically directed inwards and they differ from other natural communities. In principle they are closed communities, you belong to them, whether you like it or not.

The natural community thrives on forces that have worked for generations.

The first force is that of reproduction and associated sexuality. Generations reproduce because they have sexual intercourse and provide offspring. This force is strongly related to blood and soil. There is conquest, subjugation, pleasure, violence; it drives the continuation of our community life. In natural communities grandparents, parents and children live together. In many places in the world the people describe themselves first in terms of where they come from. Not what their work is, not their future or ambition, but first of what place and what tribe they are.

Closed communities know the power of religion and spirituality. They have a cosmic consciousness; they know their place on earth, the gods and invisible forces that accompany them, the planets that work. This force is deployed to binding effects for the community and it is expressed in rituals that accompany community moments as well as in the healing force for all physical and social ills that confront society with its fragile existence.

Sexuality and religion are not as far apart as we often think. We can see that in the natural closed community both sexual drive and religious passion play a dominant part and are interconnected. In most cases it is an adult community event in which things are expressed with gestures and gestured desires that are answered. In the worst case this leads to sexual abuse out of religious motives. The desire indulges vulnerable souls who cannot defend themselves because the other person occupies a more important place in the religious life of the community. Sects of all kind are the most extreme example.

Between sexuality and religion stands the social life that takes place in the community. Each has his role that is transferred from heredity. There are jobs to do, there is festive traffic, and all kinds of rituals are performed at important events. It channels the community being together and becoming one organism.

However, everything that is not emitted in tradition and culture is expelled from the community or the persons involved are killed. The scapegoat, the maladjusted, the idiot, the disabled, they are isolated in the community or suffer ostracism. In the natural community 'survival of the fittest' applies because of the sense that whoever adapts best also has the best chances of survival.

Leadership in the natural community plays an all-encompassing role. Everything that is there is observed, what is going on, what may or may not be, what is given meaning or what is neglected, all this is in the hands of the leaders. A central person who has gathered his paladins around him, who must perform the main tasks of leadership, exercises this destiny. The counsellor, the jester, the executioner, the householder, they all play key roles in the community and execute certain processes that are put in motion at the instigation of the leader. The leader takes all the important decisions and decides on the karma of his community members. The moral content of the leader is crucial for the way in which the community and its members decay. Is the leader a selfish tyrant or a wise person, a peace-loving man or a combating despot, a glutton or an ascetic person?

In the natural community, we go through the natural life cycle. In many societies this is still the dominant process of life, in other societies the natural community has been pushed to the background in the course of the last five centuries. There is another kind of community that arises, the organized community.

The organized community

Especially under the influence of a growing world economy in a social context that is not primarily based on blood and soil and religion but based on the rule of law by citizens who have rights and duties, a different kind of community was generated, which I call the organized community. The special feature of this community is that it is not primarily directed inward but primarily directed outward. The existence of the community is not tied to inherent sense but is connected to the service to another individual, the third person. The organized community is a target community and has a functional nature. It is aimed at achieving an output that is meaningful for someone else and meets a need. It has no natural preservation and it has no sense other than the preservation and the meaning we give it ourselves and that future generations will give it, which may or may not continue to give it meaning. That is not necessarily the case the way it is in the natural community. In the organized community "people can become persons they previously did not know they could become."

In the organized community people can work and live together for a lifetime in a way that, as members of various natural communities, would be mutually excluding each other. It is precisely the skill of this community to organize a certain new commonality. A question for leadership in this is: when does it make sense to close the organized community more and when does it make sense to open this community more. If the organized community is closed too long and intensively, similar phenomena occur to the ones we see in the natural community. It increasingly comes to using power, to the binding and tying of people to protect and preserve the status quo. The community loses contact with the outside world and is very busy with itself. This could mean that customers drop out, that employees are in a fix, that managers conceal their act. If the community is open too long, they can lose themselves in a multitude of activities and initiatives, which are then difficult to direct as a whole. Everyone is busy with their own things and optimizes its own process, but the connection is lost. There is too little in common, and energy goes into many new impulses that are not realized in the end.

A problem with the organized community is the lack of language and gesture that allow the inner world of people, the soul of the event, to be expressed. The language and gestures that dominate the organized community are the targeted functional expressions. All is put at the service of something else. Chefs steer their employees toward goals. They see their employees not primarily as fellow human beings but they see them as "human resources" that you put in or take back. In this functional orientation it is difficult for the human inner world to express itself. Personal development is only possible outside the door or in an informal context.

The organized community frees man from the jaws of his natural community but it brings man into a functional relationship between each other in which one can lose oneself. We are officers and carry out policies aimed at targets.

The Dutch philosopher Rene ten Bos deplores this.

He writes on p. 121 of his book "Stilte, Geste, Stem":

"If you choose to be united with life or with the world, then you should give up the idea of system or reason.

It indicates a desire to do everything systematically but is nothing but a lack of integrity.

A real relationship with the world is not only reasonable.

We must be aware of the affective feelings. This then means that the relationship cannot be designed or programmed.

The refusal to rule or manage the world testifies in this way of an honest attitude."

Leadership is exercised in the organized community by the management system that is operated by managers. That leadership is disconnected from people and is exercised by appointed people who are exchangeable for other people. It is a temporary thing where we can do our thing, but where at some point a farewell step should be taken. Your boss does not remain your boss, your colleagues are not your colleagues forever in the way your father is your father. However, what is striking in the leadership in the organized community is that when it comes to change, and that is usually the case, management is not able to bring this to a successful conclusion. Suddenly the persons to appear in the change process put themselves at risk. That is quite different from the functional shelter of the office and position that you have. Process owners who give themselves and who connect personally to the issue lead change processes. Then you suddenly see something else arise in the community. People meet with a common focus, connect with one another and this creates a deep trust in each other and gives each person a unique learning experience. Here the opportunity arises for anyone to step into the leadership himself, to become a leader who takes responsibility for the steps that the community is taking towards change and renewal. Here the inner world of people is addressed. Where in the operational side of the organized community everything is focused on output, in the process of change the focus is primarily on new input. Can what is new enter the company, can it be accepted and integrated. This now brings mankind further as every man is both part of the operational as of the evolving development process, which can be put down to his own leadership. This gives experiences that bring people to create their own individual community.

The individual community

Being bound in the natural community and sharing with others the organized community, this creates for man the possibility to enter into leadership. This gives him an opportunity for a fundamental different connection to himself and to his community. In the past leadership was reserved for privileged elites who by initiation or by means of a coup wanted to destine the fate of the community. Through the organized communities man has made a way for himself to come to a self-appointed place and task and existence. We are no longer tied to the natural community but have the ability to move through organized communities to a more free position in life. This now leads to people who are confronted with new questions, questions of change and renewal and development. Man himself is now in a process of personal leadership and is responsible for his own existence, his own development, but is also confronted with his responsibility to support others.

2500 years passed in which we have worked to the point that man has become an individual soul that builds his existence in a multitude of communities. We are now challenged to take a step towards others out of responsibility chosen by ourselves. I will connect with the suffering of others, I commit myself to others, and I show leadership in this. Those are the existential questions of our time and of the future. The individual steps I take in leadership and to meet others.

The encounter with others, the connection to others, the trust in others, the love for others, all this allows the creation of my own community. I will connect with other people who are not part of my natural connection, that I do not live permanently with in the organized context, but that I have a lifelong bond with and that I have chosen myself and who have elected me to be part of their community. There is no natural progress, there is no common operational goal, but there is a new form of community in which we, from a common love for an existential thing, have interconnected which connection we also nurture together.

This gives man a new conscious soul experience. I am not alone but I am with others on the way.

'I communities' play a decisive role in the future. They will pick up the new questions and bring them further. Not from convention or duty but from the will 'out of freedom to do good for others in respect to all that is.' Thus other persons also help us. Our souls school themselves at each other. This basic community power of free connected souls can engage us in the fundamental questions of our society. These are not only the questions of the suffering of other human beings, but also the question of the suffering of the earth and all its living beings, animals, trees, plants, streams, air movement, earth ground.

This touches on the fundamental theme that spiritual leaders have brought us and have held up during all ages. Buddha and Jesus gave us this issue of the liberation of the soul from their selfishness towards a basic attitude of love for others. The great philosophers have also reflected for centuries on the question of our origin, our soul and our freedom. They have entered into the question of meaning and how this can shape our own development as a human being, can give our life a sense. We can become conscious souls.

Personal leadership is an opportunity, a power and a challenge for everyone. We choose where we want it to go. Do we want to link our fate here, do we want to go this way or do we prefer to stay in the natural and organized context, embedded without wishing to be part of the leadership? This requires overcoming an existential fear, the fear of one's own existence. This also requires taking charge of one's own soul as a human being. Who or what wants to occupy our souls and the orchestration of our lives? Who or what is not involved in the encounter with others and blocks our coming together? Our own inner being can be fully occupied by the surrounding world and then the leeway is lost for the soul development. We will, all of us, go through the eye of the needle.

There is a clear relationship between the nature of a community and the nature of leadership.

In the natural community this is the hereditary leadership.

In the organized community this is the management system.

In the individual community I am the leader myself.

These three are all present in our lives. We are part of these three communities. How do we move through these three communities, how are we part of them? These are important questions that seriously determine the quality of our life.

In proportion to my developing more awareness about

- What communities play a role in my life and
- What role I play in these communities and
- How in my leadership I can find myself more in there and meet others,

It appears clear to me that, to that extent, I experience fulfilment and give the meaning of my life form and shape myself. That is the moral appeal of leadership.

Chapter 7

Leadership practice

In this chapter I want to draw on my own practical experiences over many years of acting in leadership in this exploration of our leadership hypothesis that I formulated in chapter 3.

I want to use concrete insights and experiences as a leader and advisor to leaders in various sectors of society.

My entire professional life I have worked with banks, health organizations, with government agencies and municipalities, with food chains, industrial organizations, consultancy and training organizations.

I have been fortunate in being able to work with my clients and colleagues over a longer time period at their organization development and the development of the leadership in it. I could and can follow both mainstream companies and so-called alternative organizations in many countries in a participatory way.

I will not go into all the details but I would like to articulate some conclusions of my leadership work in these different sectors of society, having worked in seven countries for more than forty years.

The World of Banks

During my 45 years of professional life as a consultant for human and organization development I have also worked with banks. In the Netherlands I worked with the major banks in the seventies and eighties of the last century. In Germany I worked and work with regional and city Sparkassen. I was also active in the supervisory board of the Triodos Bank for 14 years and now I coach the process of impulse enlivenment of this bank.

In this practice I have noticed a number of phenomena.

First of all, when banks are directly connected to their customers in a city or region, and therein finance individuals and companies, they are blessed with a long and healthy life. They fulfil their basic function in society. That is embedded in an old community principle in which the mayor, the banker, the teacher, the notary and the priest (morally) cared for the community as community leaders.

However, we see a crisis on a broad level where all these social roles come into disrepute because the authorities are not aware of their social moral responsibility.

When I look at Sparkassen but also at Triodos Bank, then it is the beauty of these banks that they formulate their goals consistently in the form of goals that will meet their clients' goals. The purpose of the bank is for its client, individuals and companies, to realize themselves. It is also attractive that these banks are still embedded in an original impulse that they monitor and always fill with new life. The Sparkassen support 'local community development' and Triodos strives for 'conscious banking of bankers and its clients'.

The big commercial banks I see drifting in the great march of civilization in which financial risks are taken so that the result, the financial profit, can be optimized.

In times of crisis it is these banks that fall or falter, not community banks. They experience even better times because the customers are once again more aware of the risks they run with their savings, assets and loans at the commercial banks.

We can conclude that the crisis is not only a financial crisis but also a moral crisis, a leadership crisis. For this purpose there are two turning points that can get us out of this downward spiral.

The first pivot is a radical change in how top leaders of banks conduct their policies and manage their business. We need moral executives who put the public interest of all of their stakeholders first and regard their organizational self-interest as of minor importance. After all, if our clients are doing well, then we are doing well.

This applies both in the short and the longer term and therefore requires a consistently implemented long-term vision of impulse drivers. This also means that no return is paramount but the client service is dominant. This ultimately leads to an efficiency that is good for the bank and its development as the facts show us clearly. If the top leaders' vision and their action-profit orientation change, then the people in the organization can also change their orientation and thus create other practices.

The second pivot is the client himself. The client can choose today with whom he / she goes into the sea. The client, i.e. each one of us, has a choice. A majority of clients act as customers that still have some confidence in traditional institutions and their leaders such as the church, the bank, the notary, the teacher, but an insidious process is going on with clients which makes them begin to think about how they themselves make their money work in society in a good way. It is the client who can decide and it is therefore essential that political leaders take up for example a distinct leadership in guiding the client's interest and client awareness, i.e. encourage their citizens to make moral choices as clients.

Eventually I see the banking crisis as a crisis of leadership and a client crisis. The leadership no longer works on a moral basis, which was the principle of the natural community, but it works as a management system on a functional basis and sets it functional goals instead of moral goals.

In addition, clients may not be aware of their personal leadership in which they can devote themselves to the good or the bad. They are still rather naïve in their decisions.

Social alternatives are now created so that we can make conscious choices. I see this as the great merit of all those leaders and communities that have rendered the innovation impulses from the sixties/seventies into social alternative institutions to enable a conscious life for all. Triodos Bank is a good example. This is a positive addition to all those negative immoral examples of selfish self-enriching responsible top leaders and their accomplices in our society.

Healthcare

In the past 40 years I have worked with healthcare organizations and also served in supervisory positions. Healthcare, that formerly very much rested on the capability of loving caregivers for patients, has now become an industry. There are many specialists in the healthcare institutes and they mainly aim at creating a treatment culture. When taking charge of their patients caregivers are faced with all kinds of procedures, rules and regulations that they should take into account. The management too quickly forgets that the customer/patient experience an entirely different process of giving meaning to their lives than they could do in their lives at home.

An example is the homes for the elderly, that clients enter increasingly late in life and where in many cases the elderly persons die in the first year of their stay. The leadership of these institutions has grown into a management system that tries to keep a grip on everything . This is also enforced by the financial interest of the government and of the insurers. Everything has to be justified, to be shown in statistics and that demands an on-going administrative effort of managers and workers at the expense of client care.

In a hospital I supported the top leader who was worried about this issue around client care. He had the idea to investigate and consider how long specific patients stayed in the hospital and why for this time period and not a different one. To his dismay there were series of cases in which nobody knew the exact answer. Patients did not know themselves, doctors and nurses did not know. He decided to have a close look every Monday morning at the actual cases that arose together with his management in order to check them and decide on the spot what should happen purely in the interest of the patient. This gave a shock effect at the hospital. Everyone was so busy with everything that the patient was more or less lost sight of. Then this director introduced a research into the various work processes and how the different departments applied them. A surgeon, who had to be operated on in his own hospital, supplied terrifying images about how he, as someone who knew the organization, experienced the lack of vision on dealing with patients:

departments did not collaborate, he had to manage his own process as a patient, make his own decisions, and insist on making that happen in the hospital. It became very clear that this hospital had a leadership problem. There was no clear guidance from the top, the managers did their thing and so did the doctors, the nursing staff was busy with their specialized tasks, thus allowing the patient to stay in bed. Each one of them felt that they knew nothing. In this hospital this problem became a theme and leadership conversations were started, based on the premise that the patient should remain in the centre of the story and how to improve this. Suddenly very big steps appeared to be possible in making this happen. If there is a mental diverter, encouraged by the responsible top leader, and people take pleasure in collaborating again so as to tune to the patient, then the difference in the process for the better for the patient and for the employee is suddenly noticeable.

In a nursing home for demented elderly people client management and client care had been discussed for years. In a conversation between director, department managers, team leaders and caregivers it appeared that, although client orientation had been much talked about, little ended up being put into practice. The pressure on nurses in recent years has increased dramatically, the protocols for all actions have been tightened, and this ultimately led to a care process which dictated tight time schedules for instance for showering patients and so on a single day they were required to shower a certain number of residents. It proved an impossible demand that led to very strange situations in the shower room. In this group dialogue it appeared that many measures of the recent past had negative effects for the client. The director thought he followed the right policy but recognized that higher echelons with different requirements overruled what he really wanted. Yet processes were put into motion in which managers and professionals were given the space to try out new practices. For example, this meant that this home moved away from meals for the whole home at the same time. Different wards could run their own program in consultation with the kitchen. This led to a lot of variety and targeted care for clients and a much more relaxed work situation for the employees.

The demented elderly man who used to rise early was not compulsively held in his bed but could get up immediately while the late rising lady on the ward could do just that. It led to a noticeable relaxation in residents and staff, better cooperation, a focused look at each resident, a surprising and joyful outcome for all, and even a more effective and efficient organization.

Especially in care we can see how good leadership works. When top leaders, managers and professionals have a genuine common focus, beautiful things can be achieved with only a few resources .

As a wonderful example of this I read about a retirement home in India with eighty inhabitants that was founded by the people themselves, in which everyone had a role and task, there was concern for each other, all the processes were done by the elderly people themselves. The result was a fulfilled community with minimal resources that was kept running for many years.

Especially in care horizontal leadership can achieve a real improvement that would make many of the measures mentioned earlier that were dictated by politics and insurers largely unnecessary.

An inspired top leader with heart for the patient and his immediate family, a collaborative management that assists all stakeholders in finding the right path, motivated caregivers and therapists who support the patients but do not take over the responsibility entirely, can lead to a viable reality for all concerned.

Government organizations and town municipalities

Our society is permeated with government organizations. These are funded and controlled by the government and should support the social well being of citizens. They are fundamental to the morality of a society. We could even say that democracy in a country can only exist if there is a proper infrastructure of government organizations. We think of an infrastructure of roads, trains, schools, cultural institutions, healthcare institutions, laws, police, and judiciary. How would a society function without this foundation? In the Netherlands we are masters in building these infrastructures. I have noticed this because of working in many other countries, where this is not so present. The Netherlands however also has an irrepressible tendency to continually reorganize all infrastructures. Presently this is happening in healthcare. From a central state healthcare we are in transition to a decentralized local government health care. The municipalities that are responsible for it now, are not quite ready for it. Towns must collaborate and they create new central bodies to arrange it for them. Suddenly all healthcare organizations have to deal with many different clients and need to see to it that their interests are secured. This causes a strain on the top leaders who need to keep their organization afloat with entirely different budgets. This can run into millions of euro's. The idea is to bring care closer to the people, but in the coming years the focus will be on the organization, the community and the institution itself.

For some years I was involved in a community in the north of the Netherlands where the municipal organization leader wanted to shake the organization up. He wanted to break the vertical structures and be much more focused and work more horizontally for the citizen. One of the initiatives was to bring all major projects in a common area. Directors of services were principals and process owners who led the projects and all processes were coordinated. Employees were involved in the processes and especially the public for whom it all was intended took part in the processes. This resulted in a great new impetus. Years of problems for civilians were elegantly addressed and resolved. Some examples: Conversion projects in neighbourhoods were aligned so that citizens met with fewer problems. Residents were able to follow a much simpler procedure for the erection and maintenance of their cemetery graves. Groups of young people who caused problems were actively invited to participate in a project in which places and situations were provided for them which made it possible to meet each other without causing problems to the citizens. In the end even the heavy engine guys took disabled youngsters for a day out on their motorcycles.

Towns provide a wide range of services to citizens. As a rule they do so very well. It must not be underestimated how complicated it is for an organization to organize a multitude of completely different services under one roof, from garbage to education, from healthcare to passport supply. There are the professionals to perform the work in large autonomy. The management is controlled in its quality of collaboration by the higher echelon. We notice that when a lot of attention is given to the meaning of the things done and to what must be changed, the processes and projects run much better. A clear communication is taking place and decisions are made on clear grounds. Each person can work independently within the common meaning of the work as a whole.

An exciting element in this field is political decision-making. Politicians have an interest in their voters being served by the government administration. On the one hand it gives a constant stress in the civil service but then issues are well raised and all matters are in the open. Thus the hybrid nature of the organization requires great driving skills of the leaders but this also results in a need for transparency. This can again propagate over-regulation and control. Leadership is an art of living in balance between development and control.

It seems important to me that the co-operation of governments with each other and with various community organizations that provide services can best be organized in a horizontal fashion. Judgment and reasoning require this. This makes increasing demands on the leadership of the top leaders, the managers and professionals.

I was once asked by leaders of organizations for disabled people to examine the possibilities of improving the process of decision making by government and service providers that influence the existence of their organization members. In a dialogical process we brought leaders of organizations for disabled people, leaders of service providers and government officials together into conversation. What was noticed is that there are two practices, one is the big house where everything happens in an organized way, and the other are the initiatives in the open field where new roads are arranged. Can those two realities come in conversation with each other; the incumbent managers and the new care entrepreneurs and enterprising people with disabilities themselves. In a major conference this was shared and this led to a better understanding of each other's issues and the role that each plays in the process. More room was given to renovation impulses but there also was a greater understanding of the uniqueness of each partner.

Such a meeting in a reflective space seems necessary at regular times as a counterweight against the functional structure that steadily rumbles in its own operational workflow.

Food chains

For years I have supervised organizations working in organic and bio – dynamic food chains: farmers and farms, producers of products, transport and logistics centres, customer shops in a chain. I have worked and still work with Ecor-Naturasi in Italy, Estafette-Odin in the Netherlands, the Wala in Germany, Rhemei in Switzerland, Terra Viva in Brazil, Anix in Siberia / Russia.

This has provided an interesting look into how to operate a chain in the current economic system. It is the trading houses that govern this chain process. They build a network of shops for the consumers, trading stores and also warehouses where the products that are bought from the suppliers come in and then are transported to the shops to serve the consuming clients. They also work together with the farmers who grow the products. Questions they face are how each party can play their role in the chain, how can we co-operate in a good way, what is the correct price that will be agreed on for each one in the chain and finally how everyone can work out of the sense of the whole. It actually begins with the end consumers who consciously choose for consuming organic and bio-dynamic products.

In Ecor-Naturasi, the fastest growing and most successfully operating organization in Italy in recent years, this chain was constructed in a few years, under the leadership of Fabio, Claudio and Aldo. Hundreds of stores throughout Italy, hundreds of suppliers processing and delivering their products, hundreds of farmers who participate in this network, they come together in the Ecor-Naturasi community. A full concentration on the core process, space and time for development of people and organization, clear procedures if something is not working, motivated owners including the original foundation as majority owner, make this work.

In a recent study we did, the farmers were found to be in the most difficult position. Less than 30% of the farmers make profits, especially as prices for their products and certainly their share in the total profits made in the chain are relatively low. Where others are doing well, the farmers come off badly. However the entire chain is based on the availability of land products produced by the farmers. How can that delivery be secured for the future? Ecor-Naturasi recently decided to reinvest a portion of its profits in the hundreds of farms that are connected to the chain. This gives a new impetus to the chain because after all many of the people/end consumers who participate care about the farmers and their fields and they find it a good thing to contribute to a meaningful fulfilled existence of all the committed farmers.

In this example, much of what is described in this book comes together.

First, the horizontal perspective, the inspiration in the top, committed managers and employees who can move, owners and investors involved in the impulse, who want to support and invest, customers who choose consciously.

At Estafette-Odin in the Netherlands the people working there do more or less the same on a smaller scale. They have now made it possible for customers to become members of the co-operation, pay a monthly fee and therefore get better prices in the stores where they buy. This brings on great customer engagement in the process, the need for clear communication in the supply chain, balancing of customer and profit interests by the directors, keeping the momentum of the organization.

In cosmetics and natural medicine the Wala Company plays a progressive role. A sublime process of growing the raw material, transforming it in an organic way to end product, sales in specialized stores with associated client treatment has been built up step by step worldwide for many years. Here again the attention to the meaning of the work, the ideal that sits behind it, the involvement of customers and employees, and the grandiose effectiveness of the products for clients, play a major role. All this requires horizontal leadership, good collaboration, clear dialogue, constantly learning from and with each other, consistency in management cooperation, proper use of the profit in the context of the foundation that manages and monitors the whole and the expression of their responsibility by the top leadership .

Rhemei in Switzerland has built a chain of bio textile products producers worldwide. Thousands of farmers in India and Tanzania grow organic cotton. This is transformed to textile products in Eastern European countries that are sold in Switzerland and other European countries as organic textiles in department stores. A small staff of people leads this entire process inspired by the pioneer owner who made it his life's ideal. If you figure out exactly how many people are involved in this chain, you will come to a hundred thousand persons. The whole chain is organized horizontally and so this is not a big company like Shell or Unilever, but it is a "little giant" who for decades has provided a formidable contribution to an organic world economy.

Terra Viva is a producer of agricultural products, flowers/plants and bulbs. 1500 people work at a twenty thousands acre plot located in several places in Brazil for a company that has existed for more than fifty years. The father and three sons of the Schoenmaker family, arriving in Brazil in the fifties of the last century as an emigrant family with eleven children, started the business. From this initiative, many other initiatives were born: from an annual flower-expo in Holambra to a bio-dynamic farm Boa Terra, from a social initiative in a favela in Sao Paulo to a syrup factory in Holambra. In the family they balance the capitalists' and the socialist's interests, as they call it. They have always been looking for value creation related to different company objectives and with that diversity in ideals and objectives the company and its people could realize their ideals into valuable fruits. They have served both the interests of the family, of the customers , the employees, and of the wider society. That is why in their view they have remained successful for 55 years. Leadership played an important role in this story. Constant attention was paid to this leadership, new impulses were sought constantly and the owners reflected on mission and vision, continuing education for all was organized and cared for. So they became a model farm company in Brazil.

Anix in Siberia/Russia was built in twenty years by its pioneer Yuri. In the region of Siberia Bisk he saw people standing in lines waiting for stores where they could pick up their products. Immediately after the fall of the communist system he started to develop his idea, which is to bring the products to the people. This resulted in 250 retail stores. Always open to new ideas such as lean management, horizontal leadership, chain development, Yuri has created a process in which all people participate in the organization and chain development. Everyone is invited to implement his ideas in their own work, like Yuri does for the greater good. This requires good coordination and consultation between many stakeholders. There they work permanently on this synchronization. Now Yuri has launched a process with regional counterpart companies from all over Russia to make a case for supermarket chains in the region, from farmer to consumer. That should provide a counterweight to the mainstream companies with violent anonymous supermarket approaches throughout Russia. Yuri and his colleague traders build entirely on the commitment of the customer, the customer experience, and the partners in the chain and are always looking for new impulses to keep this alive. Not only the product and price but also the service, the customer relationship with the supplier, and the smooth progress of the work in an effective chain, receive constant attention.

In all these examples the role of leadership, the leadership process is critical for the continued involvement of all people in the process. Everyone is accountable for his/her leadership in this approach to company development and chain development. This demands a lot from people, including much learning for all, since all people are involved in the process of leadership. It is not just the top leader who excels and tells others what to do, it is not just the management system that keeps everything together and is the driving force; it is not just the professionals

highly motivated to play their role and to contribute. It is the combi-
nation of these dimensions that leads to success and to a long-term
development especially as its own ideal in practice comes to fruition.

Industrial companies

The first eight years of my working life, in the seventies of the
last century, I worked for Shell International. As a sociologist adopted
as an experiment, I was sent to Shell companies to assist in processes
of organizational development. This was a new sport that little was
known about.

The structure of the organization was mainly one of bosses and
employees. The bosses were running the company and the employees
worked in shifts. By further specialization and the increasing pressure
from the environment on the organization to justify itself, the organization became more complex. It did not work as smoothly and simply
as it had done in the past.

Successively we introduced project work, something that was
completely new for the people, we introduced work meetings, also
completely new, and we introduced a management team, until then
unknown. This appealed to employers and employees. We introduced
social skills training for the employees. During a week they exercised
themselves in learning groups of twelve participants in elements such
as listening, asking questions, going into dialogue with others, forming
judgments. For the bosses we introduced managerial and leadership
training. In groups they pursued leadership skills conducting a difficult
conversation with an employee, negotiating with colleagues, taking a
decision. These were completely new experiences and this led the people to new challenges.

You had the Shell cross on your forehead, we said jokingly. What was
however noticed, is that in Shell in those years creative minds moved
around in the company who had a great deal of latitude where new elements were brought in and tried out. For Shell I also was such a type of

person and later as a consultant to other large industrial organizations as well. For example, in many different areas like human resources, finances, technology, public affairs, innovations were introduced and realized by these spirits. It later produced also many 'gurus' who introduced worldwide innovations in their field. Arie de Geus, a former Shell planner, who introduced a new way of scenario thinking is one example.

Later I had to deal with companies like Philips and Unilever, Esso, the Rotterdam Port Authority. Similar questions also played there. It struck me that there was a tight management culture in these companies. Each manager was tightly scheduled in the management system and had to work in it fully disciplined.

Gradually, through the shareholder value syndrome, much of the creative flexibility was cleared away. It came to much to more tight control with the aim of profit maximization. That many of these large organizations like Shell, Philips and Unilever breached their carefully built community culture and sometimes entirely destroyed it, was the price they paid. That is the work of mainstream leadership which in no way is in contact with real customers and employees anymore and has lost a feeling for the pulse of the organization, the community culture and the inner existence of committed people who have pledged their souls to the organization. This has caused much suffering and still does. It has also led to the dominant management theories based on these disastrous practices and they have thus found followers in many organizations.

Eventually organized communities have become disconnected from original impulses in many social sectors and have found an anonymous functional hierarchical management system in its place. Especially in the big companies we can experience that over many years nothing new has developed in the field of leadership and community. There is no interest beyond the preservation of one's own construct, and so there is little room for a genuine leadership development such as took place in the seventies.

In the industrial section however three new impulses in the world have yet become effective thanks to some innovative large companies, although again in time they are implemented through the traditional management mode in many companies. These are lean-organization, learning-organization, living-organization.

Lean-organization initially focuses on the streamlined operation connected to the customer. A good process flow, preventing wastage, delivering just-in-time in the chain, are impulses that should make it easier for customers and better for employees. Often, however, these ideas are used exclusively for the old profit increase purpose.

Learning-organization focuses on developing mastery and continuous education. Everybody can become a master in his profession. Creating knowledge is part of this: the freeing of individual knowledge and making this available to others who can benefit from it. However, this has in many large organizations resulted in training facilities with programs in which employees were framed in strict procedures and system requirements. Personal development was excluded, as well as the reinforcement of people's own learning and initiative power.

Living-organization touches on the sense of community building and the transfer to new generations as an essential factor for good continuity of community and organization. In the mainstream organization however, this quickly leads to various nice programs and seduction tricks to bind good employees, and the discharge of lesser employees if possible. Of course we also know the many positive effects of these three beautiful impulses in the economy and it is our view that leadership and its moral content herein is what makes the difference. The kind of effects it will have depends on the inner soul attitude that has introduced and implemented these impulses in organizations. This makes a big difference in the way they work out. It is the connection between the soul of the top leader, the soul of the management and the soul of the professional that decides the effect.

So we will have to pay much more attention to how the soul of man and of the organization have been together or not and how this connects to its leadership.

Consultancy and training organizations

When it comes to the soul of an organization, consultants and trainers play an important role. After all, they whisper new ideas and beliefs into the directors' ears. At McKinsey, KPMG, CapGemini, Boston Consulting Group, their advisers are the first partners for the top leaders. Advice mainly involves questions around strategy and structure. Top leaders allow themselves sometimes to be guided by their advisers if they themselves no longer know what to do or do not dare to do things themselves. They then send their managers to institutions like the Baak, Schouten and Nelissen, to hear about the latest news in the field of management models but also to work a bit on themselves, on their own questions and to find solutions.

There are also institutions like SIOO and university institutes engaged in the development and transfer of new impulses to professional consultants, project managers and professional leaders of social institutions. In researching and experimenting processes these new fields are being explored, new experiences and insights gained. As a teacher of SIOO and de Baak and having worked as a professor at Stenden University for eight years and now as a professor in leadership at the Hanze University I move around in these circles.

I once went to the Red Square in Moscow with a Russian colleague and I wanted to visit Lenin's tomb with him. And so we did. Then he took me to a series of graves that lie next to each other behind Lenin's tomb. "Here are the Rasputins", he said," the 'evil minds' that whispered their pernicious ideas to the leaders." Invisible to the outside world, they are the ones who actually introduced the bad ideologies; that was his idea about the Russian communist leadership history.

We can also apply this to the consulting world. Invisible advisers move in organizations to exert influence there without carrying the real responsibility. Managers tend to have a love-hate relationship with their advisers. They need them but despise them for not taking responsibility for what is eventually done, must be done. Many consultants will disappear quickly and the effects are often disappointing in the end. Advisers work only well if they are part of the leadership and involved over time in real issues that require real change from existing practices. The real adviser contributes himself and bears the consequences of his own advice given to the client.

Examination of the rules and procedures for management consultants already shows that in fact any intervention should be shunned. The consultant should stay free and should continue to advise that what he/she thinks is necessary without intervening him/herself in the existing system. The real issues, however, require involvement and will connect to making choices and these choices have to be made in practice. This asks for the leadership of the consultant, to participate and step in and take responsibility, adding something that makes the next step to be of a different quality. In particular, this applies to leadership advice. This requires a horizontal relationship between client and consultant, a person-to-person relation, where, based on mutual trust, we work together on major change and development processes. Then also the adviser demonstrates leadership and is integrated into the process. He is not on the payroll system as employee but he is recognized as a supplier for investment.

Advising leadership is a new profession. I call this horizontal leadership.

This requires a different methodology working as a leadership consultant. That is a leadership methodology.

All this we have brought together in the methodology underlying the master Leadership at the Hanze University. Together with five professors, a program manager and a team leader, we have developed a two-year accredited master in leadership where executives and professional advisers work together on their leadership, on leading the organizational development of their own team and organization. We take participants through a process along three tracks and they take the next steps.

The first track is the incorporation of new visions and stories about taking leadership from a wide range of insights in the areas of leadership, strategy development, and well-organized systems, taking control and supporting networks also in relation to the appropriate use of modern media.

The second track is personal development as a leader. In a wide range of fields such as coaching experience, intervision groups, art, meditation, participants explore their inner worlds and how they develop themselves in their leadership.

A third track is the work practice and the research studies and experiments that they take on as leaders in their work environment.

This assembly is processed into vision documents, experience descriptions, presentations and a final thesis.

It is fascinating to see how people make strides in leadership, become visible and how this contributes to a more fulfilled life of their own and of the other people involved in the process.

The synthesis

We have gone through some sectors of society and how organizations and leadership function in some concrete examples we experienced ourselves. The examples show that a fundamental consistency is needed between:

How the top leads the company on a moral basis, connected to the impulse of the organization, and with an eye for the purpose of all that we do,

How the management system works and how managers can connect personally with difficult questions and change,

How professionals, in direct contact with their clients, represent the impulse of the organization and how they can fully identify with this.

We also see reflected in the examples how precisely a lack of coherence between these three forces works out and how we then see a disconnected organization, both inward and outward, only to continue floating on the remains and after-effects of these forces from the past.

I assume that the relatively short lifespan of many organizations has to do with this disconnected reality.

Chapter 8

Leadership attitude

As a young developer of organization development I worked at Shell companies as a member of the international staff for eight years. Organizational development was a new phenomenon. The old relationships no longer worked, people were looking for new relationships. The old relationship bosses-workers was transformed to managers and employees. The old separation of functions and departments was bridged with project work. The non-communication between management and subordinates was bridged with work meetings. The breakdown in management was compensated with the formation of a management team.

In the seventies of the last century we paid attention to social skills and leadership skills. That was new. How do we deal with each other, how do we listen to each other, how do I get something done in my work meetings, how to improve cooperation with other units? Such issues were addressed in the training of social skills.

Special attention was paid to leadership. There were managers who tried to perform their management job to the best of their ability, but still little thought was given to how it could be done best. We knew Taylor with his structured organizational models, we knew Fayol with his more human philosophies of good organization, we took note of the Tavinstock investigations into employee engagement and we admired the ways of working at Volvo in Sweden with their small independent groups and greater responsibilities for these groups.

Leadership in managers we explored mainly by doing exercises and storytelling. The main story told was that of the development phases of an organization. An organization starts from the work of a pioneer, who has an idea that meets a need. He collects people around him and goes to work. Everything is done improvising. The whole is growing and at a given moment there is a crisis, there is chaos and the whole has large holes from which much is leaking. The crisis leads to interventions; we start to organize effectively and efficiently. Thus, a second phase, the differentiation phase arises, in which specializations evolve, and new departments and functions, multiple layers. There is growing management that will organize and coordinate. The whole is turned into a well-run system that can accommodate the growth. Then comes a new crisis, the creative person has been lost and we stagnate in bureaucracy, rules and procedures. We are too slow and things are too complex. This crisis we overcome if we shift our focus to the outside world of our clients. Leadership, new leadership is needed that gives the organization a new connection to the world around her. We make the organization more open and integrate it into the social events of the time spirit.

This story gave many managers perspective. We no longer are the problem and the cause of failure ourselves, we can consciously show leadership and bring the organization to development, and we can initiate change and realize it.

That was a nice thought, but how to do this?

We practiced leadership skills. An exercise we did was experiencing practicing different styles of leadership.

One style was the authoritarian style, another was a laissez-faire style, and a third was pedagogical leadership. The first two styles, so it was assumed, were practiced in the past: the authoritarian style in which the boss tells you where things are going, takes all decisions, gives others the orders and collects the results. The laissez-faire style suggested that everything will be alright in time, let things go their way, everyone does what he can do best, and as the need presents itself, we may intervene. The teaching style should provide the outcome. We as leaders consult with our people, we assist them in the work, and we tune together and share the results.

In the exercise 'building a tower' three groups were put to work with paper, scissors and adhesives to build a tower as high as possible within a given time. Each group had a leader and they were instructed by the trainers to practice a certain style. The expectation was that the group with the educational leader would have the best performance but also the highest motivation, and would have the greatest success and the best experience. In terms of work results the outcome was, however, that actually no prediction was possible. There was no direct correlation between leadership style and result. However, the people in the group were found to have an entirely different perception of the process. It is therefore not primarily the style that is right or wrong but it is the way of consistency in the process that influences the perception of the people participating. A supervisor could be authoritarian with his team and the work but still this could work very well when the boss and the team were on one line. Again, the ratio, the sense proved decisive and not the ideology.

Since that time we have been inundated with management literature that made visible in all possible ways how a manager will be successful. In essence, much of this literature is still looking for the ideal model. Furore was made by the '7s'en model' of McKinsey, the managerial grid model' dominated a period, the 'management by objectives' model was embraced, 'the transformation model' brought a new impulse, and now the 'lean' model or 'process reengineering' model is popular. In essence, however, all these models have been derived from the same ground construct; the organization is a functional-hierarchical construct, which is controlled vertically.

Leadership, however, is what makes the whole thing work well or not.

It may be a good idea to take a closer look at leadership attitude, the constant that makes the whole thing work. In our vision this makes us turn to the moral basis of leadership.

In my research on leadership and what attitude leaders radiate I have encountered a number of qualities that matter. These qualities have both the character of 'what not to do', and 'what you can do.'

What not to do!
Do not lie,
Do not cheat,
Do not complain,
Do not whine.

These are moral qualities. They reflect the temptations that leadership bring with it.

Because of responsibility and consciousness of the need to achieve results we as leaders deal with a constant pressure; pressure from everything that needs to be done, results to be achieved, interventions of all parties, busy personal lives. That brings us to the paradoxical reality of: bargaining, making compromises, cutting off the better proposals, securing one's own advantages, making use of the opportunities to escape.

Not lying is a fundamental attitude for a good leadership base that requires staying with the observation, your own intuition and your own position, and naming good as well as evil things.

Not cheating provides a basis for honesty, openness, security and safety. You can rely on the leadership process and the moral quality of the leader.

Not complaining means dealing with reality as your mentor, with that what challenges you and tells you how it stands. You look at it yourself and do not badmouth others.

Not whining means that you do not constantly bother others with your own problems and that you keep the issue in the process in which it happens. This gives light and room to breathe and to make subsequent steps.

What can you do?
Give attention in resignation,
Out of freedom trust your own intuition,
Respect all that is different
Give love to others and to their issues.

These are qualities that give stature to the soul. They ensure that the soul is not occupied but has space and time for what is substantial. This space and time in the inner world give space and time to others that are in contact with you.

They come however as qualities not just of the soul. Keeping them up requires a permanent schooling of the soul in the social reality.

Attention is given to a force that works. When I focus my attention on an issue something is going to happen that has meaning, something is going to rule. This calls simultaneously for stoicism, and for waiting full of inner tension. This active holding back is an attitude that gives birth to what wants to show itself and what can be admitted to appear. So the reality is speaking to me.

The soul will benefit from a *free space*. This freedom is connected to a consciousness of oneself, of one's role, one's place in space, one's step in time. It expresses itself in the inner response. Your own *intuition* tells you how it is and what to do. That is not logic but an inner confidence that you are connected to what is going on and that you stay connected. This gives confidence and trust between people working together. Thus we deal with the effects of our actions and let them doing the good.

We come to the others and they meet us. I can look the other person, the other soul, in the eye with *respect*, I do not need to elevate myself or to subordinate the other person. I will develop – meet – and come into contact with the other person. I appear and the other person also appears. Thus we can be on the road together.

In *love to the issue* that matters we pay attention to the issue of others, the fate that others carry in their lives. The art is to look through the eyes of the other and see where the "suffering" of the other person shows itself. We carry each other. If the other person is doing well, it is also good for me.

These considerations also include a lifelong pursuit, we connect with what we admire in great leaders that have inspired mankind for centuries by their words and actions of people that they have led to a fulfilled existence.

We think of leaders like Buddha and Jesus; we mentioned them earlier. Like many philosophers showed us all, such as Schopenhauer and Nietzsche, both are examples of leaders of mankind who show how a human being can come to leadership in his own life and existence.

Buddha

Buddha, born under a special tree under which he would die as well, bearer of many good but also bad incarnations, was destined to live as the king's son. His father wanted to keep him into his household as his successor. But Buddha left the house with a friend and first saw the old man, then the poor man, the dead man, and finally the monk without possessions and he asked the friend questions about this. This offered him a different life track. Sitting under the lotus tree in the forest, he meditated for months and he found his next step. The cobra snake protected his head from the sun. Eventually he reached a high degree of detachment and brought man the eightfold path of soul development before he took his place in the eternal life cosmos.

In this path we find mirrored the basic leadership qualities.

Leadership means developing a vision of love that helps people to take their destiny and develop their soul consciousness.

The eightfold path

Buddha expressed the eightfold path as follows:

1. Correct understanding / right views
   Understanding what suffering is
   Understanding the cause of suffering
   Understanding the elimination of suffering
   Understanding the path that leads to the cessation of suffering.

2. Right thoughts / right intentions

    Thoughts of renunciation of selfishness

    Thoughts of kindness, loving kindness

    Thoughts of non-violence, harmony and compassion.

3. Right speech

    Abstinence from telling lies

    Abstaining from speaking blasphemous language

    Abstaining from speaking harsh words

    Abstinence from nonsensical talk.

4. Right action

    Abstinence from killing

    Abstinence from taking what is not given

    Abstinence from sexual misconduct.

5. Right way of living

    No trade in arms

    No slave trade and prostitution

    No trade in living beings for meat and slaughterhouse or any other trading entities

    No trade in poison

    No trade in intoxicants.

6. Right effort

    Bad thoughts and unwholesome things that have not occurred thus to avoid overcoming evil thoughts and unwholesome things that have already occurred

    The generation and development of beneficial business and good thoughts that have not yet emerged

    Developing beneficial business and good thoughts that have already occurred.

7. Right mindfulness / right meditation (attention, awareness, concentration)

    Consciousness of the body
    Awareness of feelings
    Consciousness of the spirit
    Awareness of mental objects.

8. Right concentration

    Received wisdom, 1st transformation
    Wisdom from experience, 2nd transformation
    Wisdom from self-understanding, 3rd transformation.

This trail provides clues for what I would call the leadership motto for the development of the leadership attitude:

'In Freedom to do the good, out of love for the other, in respect to all that is'.

Jesus

Jesus was the son of Joseph the carpenter and his wife Maria. He was a special child and made already a deep impression on the scribes in the Jewish Temple as a child. When he was thirty years old, after the baptism in the river Jordan, he surrounded himself with his apostles and travelled through Palestine healing the sick, confronting the authorities.

This process started with the Sermon on the Mount.

In this Sermon Jesus made himself known to the people. He gave them guiding principles for a good and responsible life.

First he touched the human heart:

Blessed are the poor in spirit,
For theirs is the kingdom of heaven
Blessed the mourners,
For they shall be comforted.
Blessed are the meek,

For they shall inherit the earth.
Blessed are those who hunger and thirst for righteousness,
For they shall be filled.
Blessed are the merciful,
For they shall obtain mercy.
Blessed are the pure in heart,
For they shall see God.
Blessed are the peacemakers,
For they shall be called children of God.
Blessed are those who are persecuted for righteousness
For theirs is the kingdom of heaven.

You are the salt of the earth.
You are the light of the world.

Jesus did not come to abolish the law but to fulfil it.

Leadership now no longer works from rules given by top leaders but it works from the inner impulse of the man himself. No longer mankind develops out of the vertical steering of the leader alone, but we ourselves participate in the horizontal leadership between us.

A quote from the Sermon on the Mount to illustrate this:

"You have heard that it was said."

'An eye for an eye and a tooth for a tooth'

And I say unto you, resist not evil: but whosoever shall smite thee on the right cheek, turn to him the left cheek.

You have heard that it was said: "You must love your neighbour and hate your enemy."

And I tell you: Love your enemies and pray for those who persecute you.

Finally Jesus formulated the meaning of his Sermon on the Mount:

"Whoever hears these words of mine and acts on them, may be compared to a wise man that built his house upon a rock.

When it started to rain and the floods came and the house from all sides was rocked by storms, it did not fall, for it was founded upon a rock.

And who hears these words of mine and does not do like this, can be like a foolish man who built his house on sand.

When it started to rain and the floods came, and the storms raised and from all sides the house was pounded, it collapsed, and there remained only a ruin left."

Rejected by the community he fulfilled his mission to bring the spirit of Christ among men. This was achieved through suffering, destruction, death and resurrection. Leadership means the freedom to bring good among people and thereby to face evil, to confront this. It is about taking your own initiative to answer the question of another human being. In it we see ourselves as leaders confronting the process of destruction and error.

Because through many centuries until today we see these mankind leaders who provide support to the community by their moral content and this gives us a platform on which all other leaders can stand. We stand as leaders on the shoulders of our predecessors but now we take our own place.

The special feature of our time is that it is possible for anyone. Each individual can go this way and show leadership in his place and time.

We need a new moral impetus for organization and society where community leadership is concerned.

Chapter 9

The future of leadership

Now that we have examined our leadership hypothesis in different ways, from a historical perspective, from the leadership quality perspective, from the leadership community perspective, from processed insights brought by my own experience with client organisations, and from the leadership attitude, we can draw conclusions in this final chapter and outline a leadership perspective for the future.

It seems as if the outlined hypothesis in chapter 3 makes sense to us. We see the distinctive leadership coherence from different perspectives between the inspired vision of the top leader, the horizontal cooperation of management and the professionals being involved in the client process and constantly improving their own work process. When these three are in a relationship, then the organization performs and to the people in it it gives a fulfilled life. But when these three are not related, then there is a multitude of problems and tensions, cross purposes that stagnate the development of the people and the organization.

In this process of leadership it is the moral substance, the inner attitude of the persons involved that makes the difference in how leadership works in the community.

We saw the triple leadership strength at work:

Initiated top leaders who are "clear-sighted" are in touch with their surroundings providing guidance and direction;

There is a management system that not only takes care of vertically organized operations but also horizontally address change and renewal questions;

There are professionals who show their own leadership standing between customers and suppliers, owners and colleagues.

Leadership and community are related. Leaders assist communities in their development. The natural community has natural leadership; the organized community has organized leadership.

If we focus here on the future of leadership, then we concentrate on the leadership of the organized community life that we all are part of and in which we all can show leadership and on the leadership I show in creating my own community. We can be part of the leadership process, in our own life context, in our organized associations, in social events.

The important question now is how people can make this leadership their own, how to develop it, how to learn to give leadership direction to their own lives, living with others, being part of larger wholes containing their own task.

In order to make a decisive step here, we will focus on the future, on the things we have to let go and things that we have to strengthen and install. These are two sides of the coin that I want to outline here.

First the things I think we need to let go.

Things we have to let go

I see five fundamental social principles and associated practices that we would have to change radically; that we should have to let go as framework defining dimensions of socio-economic life in our society.

The first thing we have to let go is the automatic connection of being a manager and being a leader of people.

The second thing we have to release is the automatic connection of the level of education with that of the job and of the reward.

The third thing we must abandon is the hierarchical-functional top-down and bottom-up process when it comes to designing and realizing meaningful change.

The fourth thing we have to release is the automatism of employer–employee differentiation, which includes collectives on both sides.

The fifth thing we need to let go is the amoral behaviour of top leaders, managers and professionals when it comes to serving client and supplier.

The link manager – leader.

Organizations have hierarchical-functional structures containing levels of management. Briefly: top managers – middle management – basic employees. There are managers who are expected to lead their employees. The top leads the middle management and the middle management leads the employees. All systems at work are equipped on this principle. HRM systems, information systems, decision systems, consultation systems, training systems are all based on the principle that managers are the leaders of people. This however represents power relations; the higher placed person has the say over the lower. But in everyday practice the working people work almost independently of the hierarchy. The boss rarely sees his employees because he/she is too busy with his/her own problems. The manager is now deemed to give his employees guidance and does so from a hierarchical-functional power ratio. That, by definition, does not create dialogue but it leads to reconciliation at best. For example, the manager as a leader must evaluate the performance of his employee, even if he is a weak leading manager himself. Many managers dislike this leadership role and find it 'a theatre play they have to act in', that they need to force themselves into. In practice, when it comes down to it, the hares still run in different directions and they all know it

It seems much better for the future if the leadership role is disconnected from the management function. Everyone is part of the leadership and contributes to it. Everyone deserves a 360 degree evaluation when it comes to his work performance. By this I mean that the client and supplier, colleagues and the manager are all asked to give their feedback. Managers are simply professional officials as well who have their own responsibility to organize things well and they stand on an equal footing with the professionals who do the work with the client. Nonetheless, there are people who will take decisions. We can define who decides what.

When management is disconnected from leadership, I expect that much forced consultation will disappear, many useless systems will be abolished immediately, and responsible people will meet and enter into dialogue with each other in the leadership. To make this happen we will create reflective spaces and time spots to meet and discuss the real issues with those involved.

Disconnecting level of education, job and reward

If you are higher educated, you are likely to qualify for higher positions and this is linked to higher payment. All this is legitimized from hierarchical layers and more defined areas of responsibility. But in practice people at all levels can make a mess of it. It may just be the top management that by their risky unprofessional conduct brings the organization in danger. A professional can serve its customers well; the colleague is good for nothing. Well- or malfunctioning of all people runs right through the organization. This is also the case when it comes to the complexity of the work. There are many professionally difficult jobs that in comparison with the management job are a cinch for the management. Because of the far-reaching complex organizational levels, the independence of all professionals in the work process, the increased professional standards, the high demands on functional good management, because of all this we need for the future a clear horizontal structure of organizations and no longer a complex vertical management structure. Actually the basis for large wage differences between levels and functions is long gone. Is the top job much more complicated than a team leader position? The top management often acts from standard behaviour. They work with fixed indicators, the repertoire of the management work is quite in unison around the world, they are pampered and cared for, may be managers spend a bit more hours than their subordinates. If the ultimately responsible people have a good vision and this is in contact with their communities, then good leadership from the top is mostly a lot of common sense. There is no more reason to treat these people excessively. It rather alienates them rapidly from reality.

In big money-earning businesses managers and professionals benefit with the top management through high bonuses. You can see this in financial trading houses. Professionals earn outrageous bonuses as it is. This still often happens. However, we also see emptiness in the soul, people who are prisoners in the rat race, in an imprisoned context they can no longer get out of. It has an addictive effect and this is socially and personally unhealthy.

We need to set frameworks in which much more is shared with each other. First it is important to see what is needed in the game and cannot be ruled out correctly. Secondly, it is important to provide transparency of 'who contributes what' in the bigger picture. Instead of framed functions, tasks and packages of remuneration structures, we can also think of basal rewards that are proportionate to what is produced to values in this social sector. Large differences in sectors that are caused because people once more hold on to the money supply should be levelled.

Acceptable differences in pay between leaders and employees, within frameworks that are established from a social democratic process, can help us to steer extremes. The idea that we cannot do this because top talents will go and progress to better paying jobs and organizations I do not consider relevant. There is plenty of talent and capacity around in relation to what is needed. There are always people who want to get the chance to show their leadership and this process can progress quickly to what is needed in the top responsibilities.

Releasing the hierarchical-functional method when it comes to designing and achieving meaningful changes

The large numbers of failed change processes should make us alert to the question, "What are we doing wrong." In my doctoral research thesis that was published under the title "Moving organizations – the customer at the centre of our efforts" I did research on this subject. It became clear that change could not be brought about successfully along the vertical hierarchical functional lines. Change processes go under in the complexity of the event, the daily pressure, the power games, the multitude of tasks. Change processes require a different infrastructure and another methodology of work. Later I completed this process of searching for then with the publication of a new methodology in the book "Inside the Change". I called the methodology "the methodology of social evidence." The core of this methodology is that three dimensions should ensure changes to be made in the social economic life context.

The first dimension is organizing, directing and providing a specially adapted process for change that runs horizontally through the organization and in which stakeholders participate, headed by process owners from beginning to end. This requires rhythmic events in time and availability is defined in the longer term without knowing the specific activities that are intended therein.

The second dimension is that everything is done in dialogue, that is to say it is a reciprocal movement in which people help each other to take a step towards something new and try different options. There is dialogue between people who previously did not meet each other and worked together. It also affects people of different hierarchical levels and they speak personally with each other about essential issues.

The third dimension is that everything is connected with the biography of people and the organization, as it has to do with the soul of the organization and the people involved and that the people themselves are part of the process of giving meaning throughout the change process so they can connect and create trust.

This causes a different ratio between top-, middle–management and professionals.

It is mainly the professionals who need to make changes in the core processes of the organization. The managers are challenged as persons to decide if they are willing and able to lead the change process right through the organization as process owners.

It is the top that as a decision-maker is willing to take decisions on the basis of the work done by others under the leadership of the process owners. It is not the top that constantly pushes, but it is other people who bring forward the process through pulling.

Fundamental with changes is to remember that changes concern everyone, from top to bottom, from left to right. Moreover, changes not only touch on external things but it is mainly the inner changes that count and lead to new steps. If people do not admit the change into themselves, they will not appear in the outer world by taking the next steps towards something new.

Especially in change processes the leadership ability of all parties involved is essential, since the road to be searched is unknown and unpredictable events that happen must be processed. In that sense, this involves a process of leadership, a leadership dialogue, and a leadership biography.

Letting go the automatic differentiation in employer – employee, which includes collectives on both sides

Organizations divide people into employers and employees. That is a reflection of the old distinction owner – non-owner. The owner designed the fate of the non-owners. We know this from centuries of entrepreneurship. The owner should have the good moral responsibility of ownership and this is, according to Max Weber, usually associated with a religious believe in creating a good fate for life after death. A charitable relationship is the result.

Today we see in the Netherlands one million self-employed people. They are entrepreneurs and move into networks to get suitable jobs.

Younger generations do not want a lifetime bond to an organization, they do not want to be part of collective interests. They choose their next steps themselves and often have other ideals than older generations. Not the career but to be socially fulfilled is the goal, living and working with people you can trust completely is what counts.

Society turns from a vertical construct to a horizontal process. We live and work in processes and they must be cared for by ourselves more every day. Private life and business get intertwined. I have experienced this myself in my whole working life biography. It is mainly the sense question that matters in life today and this is not to be allocated vertically anymore by higher powers from above the individual. In that sense the traditional collectives, coming from different times, lose their reason for existence for the people.

It is now much more important for people to be able to take care of good life transitions themselves and they should be supported by the broader society.

A child living in a family at home transforms into an independent living and working person. From student life we move to the life of a working professional, from a full-time job we move to a part-time existence because of the family, from being an employee we move to being self-employed without employees, from a working life we move to a retired life.

Sometimes people have difficulties in making the transition. Then the broader society can help in a collective context. It is important that people do not fall through the cracks. Moreover, it is important that the broader community supports people who are disabled in one way or another, in their life destination. We can think of creating a fixed base income for all those who are in 'transition' that offers them the opportunity to make the transition in an adequate timeframe. Then we can give up all kinds of complicated vertical collective constructs that are costly and only modestly contribute when it comes down to the practical reality of people's lives. This also seems to me an essential step in the transition from the welfare state to the participative state, which in both concepts already expresses something of the social change from vertical to horizontal, which is in progress anyway in society and organizational life.

Releasing amoral behaviour of top leaders, managers and professionals when it comes to serving client and supplier

We have all, each of us, arrived at ourselves and are therefore able to see our own interests better and to ensure that this self-interest is also paramount. There is nothing wrong with that. Self-interest is required to be able to see the correct social differences and from there to seek something in common that makes sense for both parties. The dark side is that we still have great difficulty to see the limits and to determine how we deal concretely with each other. In essence, what mostly happens mentally is that everyone focuses on his own process and uses the other person in a functional sense to satisfy his own needs. In socio-economic life, however, it is practically arranged already that the interests of both parties are and must be served, as client and supplier deal with each other in the reality of life. Our consciousness however has not yet come along with this fact. We see the other person primarily as an object for the realization of our own goal.

In a broader context but also in simple concrete situations we see abuse and amoral behaviour. Demented persons are forced to stay in their beds, the customer who pays much too kindly is waved goodbye without giving notice, the speed devil cuts the old lady in her Ford in front, the CEO enriches himself based on the arrangements he has settled himself. The numerous examples bring us into a situation where the feeling of insecurity and uncertainty is building up. Although our safety and security in human history has never been so radically assured, we do not feel safe. This mirrors the moral crisis we face as people. Can I trust someone else, is the big soul question today.

On the one hand we are so tempted to join in the snatching, push in, push away the other, on the other hand we are afraid that something bad will happen to us.

The human soul seeks a balance in this tension. Some of us are busy with good charitable work, also for the benefit of our own soul experience of life.

The art of living, the art of leadership is for everyone in every situation to see the sensible thing and to do, with a view to others, the good without losing oneself.

These were all things and processes that we should let go consciously. Society is already slowly moving in this direction and when we become more aware of this we could find our own good steps more easy. This release however will ask leadership from each of us.

Now we will try to look at how the leadership of the future can manifest itself.

The leadership of the future

Based on what we have so far shown in this book we can sketch a picture of how leadership may develop in the future. I will give a first insight in how this might look. I will do this by giving an example and then by outlining the basis, the foundation for good leadership in organizations in the future.

An example

A retail organization in the drugstore market has grown into a major concern in a few years. The shops with their beautiful products work well and competition is far behind. The customer has discovered these riches and flows are increasing rapidly. This means that very soon the supply of products to the shops and also from suppliers to distribution centres is increasing in quantities that should be organized. New distribution centres are being built in rural areas. They do not just happen. In a lengthy process involving many stakeholders basically they together look at the process of realizing the new distribution centres, the meaning of everything that needs to be done, the relationships with all suppliers. The result will be a good sense making process and a design process we do together and then work can start. Throughout the process of construction the sense is closely monitored with all stakeholders as to how they can take the steps in the best way for all, why so and not otherwise. The surprising result is that these giant projects are realized within the scheduled time, with less cost than planned and function better than expected. Moreover, the people are deeply satisfied about the work that has been done together. A lot has also been learned and the people have grown in their responsibility.

Now these distribution centres are established and thousands of people work together there, gathered as a community of up to fifty nationalities. The question then arose how they will continue their work for the next few years so that the work processes run optimally, all the people in it have good lives and fulfilled working lives. This question was keeping the top management busy for a while, also triggered by the change from a two-shift to a three-shift work programme. After an intense dialogic research they came to the conclusion that actually all that is there divides the people; there are only two integrating dimensions that all share with each other: the client of the shop and the leadership process in the whole community. How can we ensure for all our clients, which are the shops and their customers, that we have the right products on the shelves of our warehouses so that we can deliver the right products to the shops on time and how can everyone be involved in the leadership for that aim, so that we all work well together? The latter was not so simple. The breakthrough in the talks came when the question was asked: "Who actually ensures that the right products are delivered to the right store, in the right time,." This appeared in the end to be entirely in the hands of the people that are at work, the employees. Then came the question: "Does this actually ask leadership from them?" "Yes", was the answer, "it is not just a routine job." So people came up with the idea to formulate for the employee, the team leader, the department head and the director what is the specific leadership quality that this role and function requires. This produced a fascinating exercise. The employee takes care of the basic process of getting the right products to the right shop in the right time. The team leader makes sure the team works well but also makes sure that it connects with other teams. The department head provides good conditions and structures, objectives and control. The director has the overview, doing proper interventions and ensures that the unit is properly prepared for and connected to the wider company context. The surprise of this exercise turned out to be that when these levels were talking to each other about their leadership responsibility, they suddenly understood each other, all got to feel how it worked for the whole. A common basis was found for conversation. This enhanced the quality of collaboration in practice but also the independence of all, the awareness of their own role in the context of the whole company.

The future of leadership could lie in the coming together of these three dimensions of leadership, leadership from the top, middle management and professionals. Then people can be working horizontally as leaders and do not need to remain in the vertical frames of rigid hierarchy and functionality. It will greatly strengthen the leadership in the organization as this leadership potential can come fully into force.

This is my answer to the growing gap between management and employees. In my book "Inside the Change" I illustrated this gap between manager and worker by describing that managers share the same question with one another and that is: "How do I ensure that my employees take their own responsibility and book their results," where employees have a common question: "When do they listen to me when it comes to clarifying the issues that we should address."

The horizontal leadership dialogue process is designated to happen in "reflection rooms" so that the leadership in the organization is strengthened and works well:

- There will be a more common perspective on what the real issues are,
- There will be a more common view on what works in addressing these issues and what does not,
- There will be a more common view how the different levels interact and collaborate and
- There will be more insight into how the organization is con-

nected with its clients and suppliers and thus the sense of work processes and policies can be strengthened.

We want to have a look now at the leadership methodology that we call horizontal leadership. Finally, we will give some tips on how this leadership can be developed in organizations.

Leadership Methodology

Our research over several decades into leadership has led to a conclusion and that is that there is no general leadership model one can apply that leads to success and results.

Leadership is based on personal capital in relation to the community, personal leadership skills are acquired that relate to the community culture in which people live and work together.

We have already described that leadership is a process in the organization community that takes place between people and where the quality

- Of the specific process,
- Of the dialogue between stakeholders and,
- Of the biographical connection,

is essential for the proper conduct of this leadership process.

We mentioned four key qualities that will be addressed in the practice of the leadership process in one way or another, that manifest themselves in situations and times and that the leader can cultivate as a leadership capacity. They can be developed into an equal and horizontal dialogue between participants.

These four key qualities are:

- Rhythmic *Steering* of a process,
- *Coaching* of learning,
- *Inspiring* with a vision,
- *Intervening* by confrontation.

Rhythmic Steering of a process

A good work process has rhythm and flow and it is focused on the contribution to its clients.

In many cases the leader is focused on content and problems to be solved. Rarely has the leader an eye for how the process works and what its faults are that hinder people to perform well. It is an art to design and organize good processes.

An example: a manager works with a management team. This team meets for 3 hours on Monday morning every week. The agenda is long and crammed, repetitive discussions take place, the meeting runs on too long, frustration among the participants is high.

The supervisor is annoyed by this bad performance of participants and actually expects different behaviour from the team members. He does everything to change this but the process is the only thing he does not change. All good intentions run into the swamp of this meeting process.

When the manager got interested in the way the meeting process was designed and started asking himself questions like 'are three hours every week necessary?', 'what themes?', 'when do we listen to each other?', he started to see that a small change in the meeting process as a process could have a big effect on how everyone behaved in the process. A meeting every fortnight for three hours, with some essential points on the agenda, led to totally different dynamics in the meeting. Each member showed more responsibility, also between the meetings, the dialogue was better and participants were listening to each other, subsequent steps were taken so that in the next meeting certain issues already looked different.

Coaching of learning

The leader can coach others in learning. By giving attention to the learning needs of the other, by listening and finding out what that person looks like after the learning step, by encouraging the other person to learn and gain, by reflecting together with the other person on the work of the learner, this can contribute to the community remaining open and the soul being strengthened. This happens especially when the manager/leader is a learning human being and is making learning steps in his own leadership.

An example: A manager notices that one of his professionals acts a bit stressed. He asks what is the matter. 'To much work', says the professional. 'Let's talk', says the manager. They talk together and it shows that the professional is struggling with the handling of a difficult project the manager gave him. 'I did this', says the manager, 'because I thought it is a good learning chance'. They agreed that the professional needs some coaching from the manager to be able to do this project in a more relaxed and convinced way.

Inspiring with a vision

When the leader occasionally shares his vision to others, he can get feedback, but also gives others inspiration and direction. Then the leader is challenged himself to connect with his own view. It is fatal if a vision is told that is not internalized. This leads to confusion and uncertainty amongst the others.

An example: A manager of a factory was preparing his vision speech he holds every year at the start. He tries it out to a colleague. 'Totally boring', the colleague says, 'nobody will be listening'. 'Why don't you tell it like you tell it your 15 year old son'. The manager tries. 'Wonderful', says the colleague, 'do it like this'. The community is surprised and delighted when they experience the speech. It leads to lively dialogues the next weeks.

Intervening by confrontation

Managers/leaders often have to confront and stop projects and activities. Mostly from good intentions they want to allow others to do something that is dear to them, they do not want it to take it away from them, they do not want to hurt them, they want them to stay as they are.

However, in the end this leads to a-social behaviour and makes social relations problematic. It creates a shadow and it generates confusion and misalignments.

An example: A team leader is frustrated by the performance of one of his professionals. The clients are complaining about the way they are treated by the professional, but the colleagues like his unorthodox behaviour especially opposite the higher management. The team leader decides in the end to confront the professional with the response of the clients. The professional is shocked by the stories of the team leader and starts to defend himself. This ends in a discussion that in the end the team leader stops. 'I will come back to this', he says to the professional. A week later they meet again and the team leader asks the professional if he spend any thoughts on the client complains. 'I slept bad from it', he says, 'but I must see that there is some sense in what you say'. 'Clients are not my bosses, I should be I guess a bit less aggressive and give them better service'. The team leader suggests they see in two month if this intention worked out in the practice.

These core competencies are part of a methodology for leadership. They take place in a good process, in the dialogue, in the biographical connection.

However, this should be supported by a scientific inquisitive attitude. We can deduce this investigative leadership attitude from the inquiring attitude shown in natural science and spiritual science .

Natural science asks two qualities of inquisitive attitude of us:

The first quality is that we remain in the observation, *the phenomenological attitude*. We constantly have to return to the observation, always observe reality from an active involvement in this reality that we examine. In examining reality, it will be moved, it develops, changes, metamorphoses. What yesterday was, is different tomorrow. Through continuous observation of and dialoguing with the question owner, that question that we investigate is moving and changing. The issue comes to life in those affected and calls on them to act, to take a next step.

The second quality is that of continuous assessment, *the empirical attitude*. In social reality we continually check with others how they see the question. How is that question alive, do they observe the same? We test our findings with others and do it again and again so as not to lose sight of the differences. These differences unfold the multiple dimensions of the problem; the problem is not an objective thing but, after all, is bound to the social constellations that have to do with this problem.

Spiritual science also requires two qualities of us:

The first quality is that of listening to the stories that move people, *the narrative attitude.* In the stories of people involved we hear the meaning of things, how people sense and indicate what they encounter along the way and we get closer as researchers to what moves people inside. Where we were once part of great stories, we now together create stories from our individual experiences. So we are connected through stories with the social reality in which we act as researchers.

The second quality is that of the awareness of our steering convictions, *the symptomatology attitude.* We live with views that we have created in our own lives that we have made. Transferred by others, related to values we share, they guide our behaviour in situations. When we make ourselves aware of them by observing the effects of our actions on others who act, we come to conscious choices about what it is that leads us. Thus we gain insight into patterns of life and how we can move with them and change them.

So we move ourselves in a great social perspective when it comes to an investigative leadership attitude. It is not a distant looking for general laws, as this may apply to nature and spirit by the research scientist, but we are looking for something in the social work and do this by participating in this actively inquiring process out of leadership. This development brings us deeper into the realities where we stand and that we can metamorphose into a growing social and moral consciousness that arises in us and between us.

So we all become inquisitive leaders.

This inquisitive leadership now requires the creation of reflective spaces, reflective dialogues and processes, in which involved people can participate. This is the core task of leadership: the creation of these reflective spaces and processes. The involved people can work on their sense making and thereby bring the social ability to a higher moral level.

Thus we finally come to our eight tips for leadership.

Tips for leadership

These tips are in a sense a summary of this book.
They consist of powerful statements that I often hear myself say when I work with leaders on questions of leadership.

Tip 1
Leadership is not doing anything ourselves, but setting up a good process in which others can act.
Leadership requires a certain intelligent laziness. A good leader does not seize everything to himself, does not always take the lead, does not take any burden on his shoulders that belongs to others, does not take over all monkeys that sit on shoulders of others, does not always take care of others, but creates the conditions in space and time that enables others to act, to take responsibility, to take initiatives themselves and to realize them. Cultivating a reflective attitude, an active reflective attitude in yourself, creates this intelligent laziness. With Heidegger and Meister Eckhart one can say: an attitude of attentive waiting. By attentive waiting one can express oneself in the substantial duration of processes that take place in us and among us.

Tip 2

Leadership is questioning the youngest person when it comes to questions of the future, because the youngest soul can express the essence because he is still closer to God.

This is inspired by the rules of Benedict that he set for his monk community, a set of rules that may still have significance today in organized life and community. They are actually leadership rules for a life of "ora et labora", "work and pray", of "act and reflect." The past we can examine and give meaning, but the future is a surprise. Many things come back and go on but they are always slightly different the next time. The past stands before our eyes, but the future does not stand before us but approaches us from behind, we can hear the future. Sometimes the future takes us by surprise, sometimes it comes gently. In the young souls that live in our community the future can speak out and it is the very young people who can contribute a lot to getting a feeling for the future. Let us not keep young people waiting until they are older but let us as leaders encourage the leadership of youth by involving them as the first in questions of the future. Older people may be asked to reflect on the contribution of young people and to provide an enhanced meaning.

Tip 3

Leadership is addressing the meaning of the case, asking the why question and to what use, also taking decisions carried by values that meet real needs of others.

As leaders we are busy with all the things that come by. We are captivated by the 'what' and 'how' and should ensure that targets are met. Others also like us to be obvious leaders. Then we have our own act together. Yet it is the leader who has to ask the question of meaning, not only afterwards if something went wrong, but before, during and after the current process. This is most reflected in the decisions I make as a leader. Acknowledging others in my decisions, I can clearly communicate these decisions because others know me and know the values associated with our business momentum. A primary focus of the leader here is to investigate if what we always do meets the needs of others for whom we are there.

Tip 4

The leader opens the door through which we can enter into new areas and he closes the door after we have said goodbye.

The door or gate is a beautiful symbol of leadership because it symbolizes the transition from one space to another. What doors do we have in space and time that we can go through and what doors we would like to close behind us? Leadership is also saying goodbye, finishing so we can enter new areas. Opening a door to a new area starts with the leader in the inner self, the soul. In this leader's soul questions are said farewell to and new beginnings start. If the leader holds both doors closed, there may be no room for change in the organization, for both processes, saying goodbye and making a new start, are blocked. The leader himself opens the doors in the encounter with the unknown, the strange, the different. This raises questions and those questions we will discuss. It will be the leader who has the right intuitions and comes to good decisions.

Tip 5

The leader reflects the community and sometimes directs the community rhythmically by connecting the community to the inside focus and sometimes opens the community to gaze out.

When a community has been closed for too long, it will start to experience all kinds of unwanted processes between people. Abuse of power, violence, sexual abuse, harassment, all this involves having to deal with fear, hate and guilt. If the community has been open for too long, then it blows away everything and goes in all directions, loses its coherence and this is accompanied by feelings of frustration, discouragement, and futility. Proper rhythmic alternation of opening and closing the community by the leadership helps the organization as a community organism to be endurable and able to find its own way. Speed is a bad counsellor for this. It is really better to slow down the questions that are in marshy areas and to strive for this rhythmic alternation. This requires of the leader an open eye for the actions to take, his guidance and having an open ear for feedback.

Tip 6

The leader combines professional expertise with disciplined self-organization and with his ideals in life.

Good leaders are well versed in the communities they lead. They understand the business, have a sense of the core process of the organization, are at home in support processes, so they have a wide experience and at the same time they are very disciplined in their actions, they are focused, they act fired by their own ideals. These ideals are eminently focussed on the fortunes of the others. It is the leader who is not focussed on himself, but he is concerned with the others. Therein, however, the leader is entirely connected to himself. The leader is always willing to learn, to learn new elements of the trade and 'the property' of 'the business', without wanting to play the expert. He also directs his own life and does not permanently hang on and around others.

Tip 7

The leader has his sparring partners who cast things back at him and support him.

Being a leader is lonely; it all comes down to yourself in the end. This asks of the leader to connect to other people who you can trust as a leader and who are willing to cast things back to you and support you. Trust is based on connection that is born of a common focus on what matters. Confidants are not fast and they do not depart quickly. It takes time to build that trust. It is like friendship. Even that is not a short-cycle-life thing. It can last a lifetime. It is important to have an eye for who your friends are, who your confidants are, who really care for these relationships so that they are two-sided and not one-sided.

Tip 8

The leader knows when his time is over, when to come to the decision to go and give space to a successor.

Leaders must not linger when their time is up and over. They sometimes have the tendency to organize everything around themselves only focusing on maintaining their own position. A whole community may be sacrificed by this attitude. Choosing the right time to leave gives space to others to step in. In most cases it is also better not to want to allocate one's successor. It is the others who travel further and must take care of continuation, and they should find a successor. A dignified farewell shows the fruit of one's own work and one's work in the community that one, sometimes during a long time, has served.

The leader is looking for his next step, which usually presents itself if he has an eye for this.

Finally

Thus we come to the end of this book. Leadership is a mystery, a mystery of community. It is connected with ancient questions about our origins, our soul, our freedom or intended, moral questions. Leadership touches the heart of existence. It is an existential question, an existential process in which we can stand up as man. Each of us, who wants to, can be part of the leadership process.